TOGETHER FOR EVER

GOD'S MASTER PLAN FOR MARRIAGE

Together For Ever

TOGETHER FOR EVER

GOD'S MASTER PLAN FOR MARRIAGE

Victor & May Victor

| Together For Ever

All scripture quotations unless otherwise marked are taken from the New King James Version of the Holy Bible. Copyright © 1979, 1980, 1982, Thomas Nelson, Inc., Publishers

Scripture quotations marked as Contemporary English Version® are taken from the Contemporary English Version, Second Edition. Copyright © 2006 by American Bible Society. Used by permission. All rights reserved.

Scripture quotations marked Amplified Bible are taken from the Amplified® Bible, Copyright © 1954, 1958, 1962, 1964, 1965, 1987 by The Lockman Foundation. Used by permission. (www.Lockman.org)

Scripture quotations marked The Message are taken from *The Message*. Copyright © 1993, 1994, 1995, 1996, 2000, 2001, 2002. Used by permission of NavPress Publishing Group.

Copyright © 2012 by Victor & May Victor

Printed in the United States of America

No part of this publication may be reproduced, stored in a retrieval system or transmitted in any way by any means, electronics, mechanical, photocopy, recording or otherwise, without the prior permission of the author except as provided by USA copyright law.

DEDICATION

This book is dedicated to the Holy Spirit who taught us God's Master Plan for marriage and made writing this book possible for all those who desire a together forever marriage.

Together For Ever

ACKNOWLEDGEMENT

With special thanks:

To our parents thank you for being a good example to us. They enrolled us in the first university of marriage without asking for our permission. It is their idea of marriage that the Holy Spirit modified according to God's divine plan for marriage.

To our children, Stephanie, Victor Jr and Tochi for enduring the late nights and the awkward lifestyle that made writing this book possible. Now you know why we went to bed early and woke up early.

To Dr. and Mrs. Emmanuel Okorie, thank you for showing us early in our marriage how to build a Christian home. The lessons of those years are the landmarks of our life as a family.

To Pastors Toye and Wumi Ademola and to our other families at Dominion International Center in Houston Texas, thank you for the opportunity to minister to the young ones. By so doing we renewed our strength and receive enlightenment.

To our friends at Two-gether for Ever Marriage Ministry, thank you for being our friends. We set out to teach the principles of marriage, but we become students of your wisdom, knowledge and enduring commitment to the institution of marriage.

TABLE OF CONTENTS:

PART I: Understanding Marriage

Introduction

Chapter 1: What is Marriage?

Chapter 2: Finding Your Wife

Chapter 3: Biblical Models for Finding a Wife.

Chapter 4: Modern Day Trends in Finding a Wife

PART II: Before You Get Married

Chapter 5: The Wonders of Premarital Counseling

Chapter 6: The Wonders of Effective Courtship

Chapter 7: Group Association/Peer Bonding

Chapter 8: Role of Models and Mentors

PART III: Now That You Are Married

Chapter 9: The Four Phases of a Marriage Relationship

Chapter 10: The Art of Staying Married

Chapter 11: Communication Skills that Work in Marriage

Chapter 12: Sex is God's Idea

Chapter 13: Money and Your Marriage

Chapter 14: Maintaining the Family Altar

Chapter 15: Dealing with Third Parties

PART IV: When Marriage Fails.

Chapter 16: What the Bible Says About Divorce

Chapter 17: Picking Up the Pieces

PART 1

Understanding Marriage

Together For Ever

Introduction

Marriage in the Plan of God

Marriage is the cornerstone of God's master plan for His creations. God created a perfect world and felt good about the work of His hands but there was no caretaker for the newly created estate. He then created man in His image to manage the estate and propagate it into eternity. We see in Genesis that man was giving unlimited authority to rule the earth. The first instruction that God ever gave to anybody or anything was given to Adam and Eve jointly.

Then God blessed them, and God said to them, "Be fruitful and multiply; fill the earth and subdue it; have dominion over the fish of the sea, over the birds of the air, and over every living thing that moves on the earth" (Genesis 1:28).

This was a turning point in the relationship of the Creator and the creation because prior to this instruction God's communication with His creations was declarative. "Let there be... And there was ..." The sea and the animals did not play any role in their wellbeing but simply obeyed the orders.

But when He addressed Adam and Eve, the language became instructive and affirmative as in "Be fruitful and multiply..." This choice of language was not an accident but a deliberate acknowledgment of man and his role as a co-creator, an announcement of this relationship to other creations and finally the coronation of man as the dominant creation.

It must have been this thought that overwhelmed the Psalmist when he cried out aloud, "What is man that You are mindful of him, and the son of man that You visit him" (Ps 8:4).

These words were both an acknowledgement of the elevation of man above other creations and affirmation of the role of man in his own manifestation. Man was to a very large extent the master of his faith and the captain of his soul just like God.

Even more significant for our purpose here is the fact that the affirmations and instructions were given to Adam and Eve jointly, perhaps indicating that Man's strength is maximized and enhanced when complemented by his wife's strength. This means that you are at your best when you are working with your wife. Your destiny is secured, your distance is shorter and your obstacles are surmountable.

It is significant to remember that Woman was not part of the original plan of God. The original plan was to make man in the image of God and for man to have dominion over God's creation. But God decided to change that plan. "And the Lord God said, "It is not good that man should be

ALONE; I will make him a HELPER COMPARABLE to him" (Genesis 2:18).

Everything God made in the beginning was good. Man was made complete and good. The only thing 'not good' about man was his 'aloneness'. The word 'Alone' means the following:

   a. Exclusive of anyone or anything else
   b. Radically distinctive and without equal
   c. Isolated from others
   d. Lacking companion and companionship.

A helper is one that contributes to the fulfillment of a need(s) or the furtherance of an effort or purpose. A helper aids, assists and supports the pursuit of a project, the realization of a vision, and the fulfillment of a destiny. Man and woman need each other for the fulfillment of their assignment in life. Without one, the other is short circuited and alone.

Furthermore, the use of the word "comparable" in that scripture indicates that the woman (helper) is capable of being compared to the man; of having features in common with the man, and suggests equality with the man. Notice that God did not just call the woman into being. He made her the same way He made the man which is in God's image but from the man's rib. So that she will have a connection to both God and man.

Perhaps God saw the challenges of the work to be done by man and added reinforcement to help man accomplish it.

Because God is a wise God, the Helper that God made brought with her everything that is not good in man.

And so God created a helper that is like man in many ways to complement him, but unlike man in many ways to spice up the isolation and boredom. Above all the helper will complete man in furtherance of man's purpose. This was the heart and soul of the union between Adam and Eve.

Today's marriage is the continuation of that divine union that is part of God's master plan. This is why all Christians should understand that any attack on their marriage is a frontal attack on the plan of God.

Until we fix our marriage base, the church, the community and the nation will continue to experience the consequences of broken homes, fatherless children, single parenthood etc.

Chapter 1

What is Marriage?

And He answered and said to them, "Have you not read that He who made them at the beginning 'made them male and female'... (Mathew: 19:4).

Marriage is the state of being united to a person of the opposite sex as husband and wife in a consensual and covenant relationship recognized by law. (Webster Dictionary). The word "marry" is derived from the French word "Merrier" which means to marry.

Marriage is the first institution established by God solely for the advancement of His kingdom. It is designed to be a permanent fusion of two individuals (body and soul) into one for the pursuit of one destiny and therein lays the mystery of oneness.

For this mystery of two becoming one to happen, the man has to leave his father and mother and cleave to his wife. The word "cleave" is derived from an old English word "cleofam", which meaning includes:

1. To pierce or penetrate

2. To penetrate or pass through something, such as water or air
3. To adhere, cling or stick fast
4. To be faithful.

God does not expect only loyalty in marriage but oneness; He does not expect only faithfulness but love. When two become one there is no need to be loyal because you are one. In that oneness the interest is unified, pursued and protected. It is a lack of understanding of the purpose of marriage that creates avenues for unfaithfulness, disloyalty and adultery.

The commitment to marry anybody is a huge responsibility. A man and his wife have to consummate the marriage, adhere, cling or stick fast to each other for them to initiate the process of becoming one.

Marriage is the only covenant that requires the parties to lose their individual identity in exchange for the union's identity. Under the marriage covenant, the parties primarily surrender their rights and privileges to the union. By choosing one partner from the many options available, the couple inadvertently:

1. Announce their CHOICE of each other;
2. Announce their EXCLUSIVITY;
3. Announce the end of the SEARCH for a partner;
4. Pledge to find COMPANIONSHIP in each other;
5. Pledge to PROCREATE only through each other and

18

6. Promise to make the union PERPETUAL.

Each of these commitments is undoubtedly turning points in the life of a young man or woman. The implication of these decisions can reverberate through the lifetime of the parties. Get it right here and coast through life. Get it wrong here and life becomes a grind full of regrets and clogs.

Unfortunately many enter into marriage driven by testosterone and oblivious of the cost of the commitment and certainly unaware of the finality of marriage. Like death, one can safely say that it is appointed unto man to marry once and after that stay married or live as a single person. It is surprising how many young men are unaware of the power of their sexual drive. If you allow the desire for canal expression to be the sole reason for marriage, then the marriage is doomed because sex alone cannot sustain the relationship.

I once watched a documentary on the life of elephants in the African plain. In that documentary, two bull elephants fought for two days nonstop for the right to mate with the female herd in the Ngoro-Ngoro national park in east Africa. At the end of the second day, both elephants were bruised and battered. One elephant had a broken tusk while the other had a bleeding cut on his right ear. The elephants fought unconcerned about their surroundings, and unconcerned about food or water. Such is the power of our mammalian sexual drive.

Although men have tamed that drive to a large extent, the underlining pull is still very strong. Many are still entering into marriage commitment based on physical attributes alone; yet, nothing should be further from truth.

Chapter 2

Finding Your Wife

There is a man or woman for everyone who desires to be married. This is because God has already declared that it is not good for man to be alone. Your challenge is to find one. God almighty has ordained that whoever you decide to make your wife will add value to your life by bringing favor to your life. Your stock increases the moment you find a wife to marry. "He who finds a wife finds a good thing And obtains favor from the Lord." (Proverbs 18:22).

Conversely there is a wife or a husband that God has set apart for you. I am talking about your soul mate or your missing ribs in the true sense of it. In him or her is your destiny fully maximized and your favor from the Lord optimal. Your challenge is to discover the person or allow yourself to be discovered and accept each other.

"And the Lord God caused a deep sleep to fall on Adam, and he slept; and He took one of his ribs, and closed up the flesh in its place. Then the rib which the Lord God had taken from man He made into a woman, and He brought her to the man. And Adam said:

"This *is* now bone of my bones
And flesh of my flesh;
She shall be called Woman,
Because she was taken out of Man" (Genesis 2:21-23).

Adam recognized Eve as his wife from the beginning and immediately defined her role in his life. Many who have found their wives just found her without equivocation while others who set their eyes on lofty goals have missed their wives right under their nose.

More often than not, she is not your model wife and you are not her dream husband. You are likely to discover each other when you are not searching or where you least expected it. Unless you have learned to hear and obey the Holy Spirit, your first reaction may be to suppress the thought or reject the initial advance. You may not even be satisfied with the choice at the beginning but eventually the reason for your union begins to unfold. Put simply, she or he "may not be your type". Nevertheless, there lies your fulfillment and the easy road to the completion of your assignment in life. Great unions always get better with time.

Leah was not Jacob's choice for a wife. In fact Jacob was not happy that his father-in-law gave him Leah for marriage instead of Rachel. He was so much infatuated with Rachel that he worked another seven years for the permission to marry Rachel. But it is obvious that Leah was God's choice for Jacob because God's plan was fulfilled through Leah. The lineage of King David and our Lord Jesus Christ is traceable to Leah. On the other hand, Rachel, who was Jacob's personal choice turned out to be barren for a while, and ultimately died prematurely (Genesis 29). But this does not mean that it is wrong to marry for love. Finding love within God's plan for your life is the ideal situation.

In chapter three of the book of Ruth, we read about the fascinating story of Ruth and Obed. In this story Obed was persuaded to marry Ruth and by so doing preserved his destiny in being counted among the lineage of David and Jesus Christ. David married Bathsheba the widow of Uriah, yet it was through Bathsheba that he preserved his destiny through Solomon. "Then David comforted Bathsheba his wife, and went in to her and lay with her. So she bore a son, and he called his name Solomon. (II Samuel 12:24). God certainly does not see what we see.

The fact is that no matter how much we try, most of us will marry a wife and not the wife that God reserved for us. This is because man judges by the outward appearance but God judges by the heart. The good thing is that whether you marry a wife or the wife, there is a special favor for you. My prayer is for you to find the wife that God has designated for you so that your destiny will be fulfilled. For those who have to find a wife, the wife you find will determine the distance you go in achieving your destiny. The closer your choice of partner to the choice of God, the better you are in finding the team mate for the game of life.

How do I find a wife?

The process of finding a wife should start with a clear and concise definition of who your wife is. Although most of us have an idea of what the term "wife" means, what we want in a wife or husband is very subjective and often dictated by several factors. Even people of the same faith and belief have their own idea of who a husband or a wife ought to be.

For Adam, a wife is a HELPER to carry out the responsibilities that God committed into his hands. Eve was taken out of Adam's body and that also reflected on the closeness and oneness. Adam's wife had to be a mini Adam ready and able to act for Adam in his absence. In this sense Eve had to have the ability to do some of the things that Adam could do. Like Adam, some men prefer a woman who can take care of their family in their absence. Many who are called into pastoral ministry deliberately look for a "pastor's wife material". A woman spiritually matured, fiercely loyal, strong and able to command respect from the congregation.

These women are usually strong willed, highly educated, self motivated and confident in themselves but all these qualities are tempered by the fear of God. The men who search for such women are interested in the undisturbed continuation of the family unit or business whether they are there or not. This is often a union of two strong leaders ensuring a strong and respectable family. In this union decisions are primarily made jointly between the man and the woman. Some families include their children in decision making.

Ultimately the success of using this value system to find a wife is dependent on the management of the two giant egos. Egos are managed primarily by the understanding of the roles and responsibilities of each member of the union. When the man understands that certain matters are the responsibility of the wife and respects the choices that she makes in carrying out those assignments, the couple will avoid conflicts. The woman understands that her choices affect the family and that her husband is ultimately accountable to God and the society for the outcome of his decisions.

The couples with better understanding of the roles in the family are very likely to succeed with less friction. The man may appear less dominant, sometimes even weak and lacking authority. But what he sacrifices in power, he gains in strength from the decisions that are made in committee with his wife.

Eve was also expected to complement Adam in areas of Adam's weaknesses. This means that whatever Adam lacked, Adam's wife is supposed to have in abundance to make the team of Adam and Eve formidable. If Adam was tall, Eve was supposed to be short to bring the advantages of shortness. Some men and women start the process of finding their wife with this in mind. A few years ago a man surprised his friends by marrying a woman who is almost one foot taller than him. Today that marriage is successful because the man's need for a wife was someone who will at the very least complement his height challenge.

It is said that "He who finds a wife finds a good thing, And obtains favor from the Lord" (Proverbs 18:22). . Historically, men and women have used various guides in their search for a suitable life partner. Some of these criteria include:

1. Companionship
2. Procreation
3. Continuation of a blood line
4. Love/Passion
5. As a means of building alliance; and
6. Economics

Chapter 3

Biblical Models for Finding a Wife

Whatever the value system used by the finder, a wife adds value to her husband and a husband adds honor to his wife. We will now look at various biblical marriage models and the principles behind them.

Isaac's Model

The value we place on marriage determines the kind of wife we search for and where we search. Isaac's search for a wife was the first recorded example of a search for a life partner. At the time of the search Sarah, Isaac's mother was dead and Abraham was well advanced in age. The only interest of Abraham was to ensure the continuation of the blood line; a king ensuring that the dynasty does not derail from his family and the bloodline does not get corrupted.

Isaac was the promised child that was to carry on with actualizing the promise of making Abraham and his descendants a great nation. We are not told of any other consideration. We are also not aware that Isaac played any role in finding his wife, Rebekah. The decision was made by

Abraham and his trusted servant. Obviously this was acceptable to God because He affirmed this in Exodus 34:16.

Abraham's interest was therefore specific - the preservation of the blood line and the exclusion of the Canaanites from his lineage. His guideline (search criteria) was clear and concise, leaving very little margin for error (Genesis 24:1-4). Abraham's trusted servant will have to mistake another city for the city of Nahor, Mesopotamia, and another family for Abraham's relative to miss this assignment.

Well defined criteria for your search will save you wasting precious time and suffering unnecessary heartache. You will avoid wandering from Cape to Cairo and still wondering whether your current fiancé is "the one." Define your criteria, express your intentions and compare notes with your prospective partner. Is he or she going where you are going in life? What about time? Is he ready to leave or is he leaving in two years time and you are already at the bus stop? Even if he is ready to leave, is he flying or taking a greyhound bus? Align your criteria and you will eliminate guess work.

Isaac's model appears to be God's model for your search for a life partner. Some begin there and add other methods since God has on various occasions affirmed the principle and even justified the reasoning (Exodus 34:16-18 and Deuteronomy 7:3-4).

"Nor shall you make marriages with them. You shall not give your daughter to their son, nor take their daughter for your son. For they will turn your sons away from following Me, to serve other gods; so the anger of the Lord will be aroused against you and destroy you suddenly." (Deuteronomy 7:3-4).

Today this is still prevalent in arranged marriages where parents and communities are only interested in the preservation of the bloodline. The desire to marry from a particular race, tribe or nation, is placed above the need for companionship, compatibility and overall suitability. Isaac's model is now God's acceptable model from the time of exile in Egypt to the time of Paul in the New Testament. Whether the instruction is "you shall not take their daughters for your sons" as in above or "Do not be unequally yoked together with unbelievers" (2 Corinthians 6:14), the application is the same. It is still the law of the land for the followers of Christ!

Jacob's Model

While Adam's wife was presented to him, Jacob had to discover his wife by actively searching for her. There was a clear and concise instruction of what Jacob should be looking for. Clearly the preservation of the blood line was important to Isaac and Rebecca, but Jacob's personal interest was companionship/love. Here we see the interaction of the quest to preserve the bloodline and the need for companionship.

The ideal wife for Jacob had to come from his parent's kindred and had to be attractive to him for companionship. Jacob followed instructions in his search by going to Laban,

Rebekah's brother in the Land of Padan Aram to search among his cousins. Rachel provided companionship but it was Leah that preserved the linage of our Lord and continued the promise.

"Then Isaac called Jacob and blessed him, and charged him, and said to him: "You shall not take a wife from the daughters of Canaan. Arise, go to Padan Aram, to the house of Bethuel your mother's father; and take yourself a wife from there of the daughters of Laban your mother's brother.

> "May God Almighty bless you,
> And make you fruitful and multiply you,
> That you may be an assembly of peoples;
> And give you the blessing of Abraham,
> To you and your descendants with you,
> That you may inherit the land
> In which you are a stranger,
> Which God gave to Abraham." (Genesis 28:1-4)

Esau's Model

Esau desired a wife for companionship and recreation. Therefore Esau's wife had to meet only one standard - appeal to Esau' eyes. It did not matter where the woman came from, what her beliefs were, the cultural differences, the color differences, the language, the nationality, the blood line, as long as the woman was good looking and compatible with Esau. This is the trophy model and unless you are a king with several wives this is a wrong way of choosing a spouse and the consequences are far reaching. The bible says that Esau's choice gave his parents Isaac and Rebecca grief.

"When Esau was forty years old, he took as wives Judith the daughter of Beeri the Hittite and Basemath the daughter of Elon the Hittite. And they were a grief of mind to Isaac and Rebekah" (Genesis 26:34, 35.).

King Solomon was not interested in preserving the blood line. We know that most of Solomon's wives were the daughters or relatives of kings from other nations. He used marriage to build political alliances with his enemies and enter into treaties with his allies. The bible records that his reign experienced the most peaceful time in Israel's history. There was economic progress and the nation of Israel was reckoned as a powerhouse.

We also know that Solomon's reign witnessed a period of spiritual stagnation and idolatry in Israel. Solomon gave his wives, from other nations and religion, the freedom to worship the gods brought from their families and countries. He even allowed them to set up shrines and proselyte their religion in Israel. The women turned his heart away from God. This was exactly the reason why god instructed them not to marry from other nations.
"For they will turn your sons away from following Me, to serve other gods; so the anger of the Lord will be aroused against you and destroy you suddenly" (Deuteronomy 7:4).

The effect of the adaptation of this model was a shift in the destiny of Israel. The consequence was more grievous than the grief of Isaac and Rebekah because the nation of Israel as we knew it came to an end. The kingdom was divided during the reign of his son Rehoboam and ultimately destroyed by other nations. The Israelites were carried away to other nations.

There are also success stories of inter-racial/inter-cultural marriages or marriages across the blood line. The success of such marriage depends on the willingness of the spouse to accept the new people, culture, faith, language and residence. Ruth is a prime example of an inter-cultural marriage that was successful and blessed.

In 1977, a young catholic woman traveled to a foreign land and fell in love with a Muslim man. His people spoke a different language, had a different culture and lifestyle. The catholic woman later married the Muslim man, converted to Islam, changed her catholic name, changed her wardrobe, learned the language and embraced the culture. To show her devotion to her husband, she visited Mecca and Medina and became a devout Moslem. Today, that marriage is blessed with several children; the woman is well respected in that nation and has even held several government positions in the nation. Although this was sad that a Christian abandoned her faith but it is very illustrative of what inter-racial and inter-cultural marriage must do to survive and thrive.

The story of Ruth is an interesting one here. Ruth a Moabite left her pagan religion and heritage to embrace her husband's people and their way of life. It offers a lesson in true love, devotion and ultimately preservation of a destiny that was in danger of extinction. For her faithfulness God honored Ruth with the privilege of being in the lineage of first King David, and later our Lord Jesus Christ.

Today love and strong devotion remains the key factors that make inter-racial, inter-culture, marriages successful. Couples that have isolated themselves may appear successful but often lack that true identity and direction to endure beyond the first generation.

The bible has provided a laundry list of the values that a good wife brings to her family. The values can be summed up as follows:

1. She is a trusted companion of her husband causing her husband to trust her.
2. She is a HELPER and a defender of the family complementing her husband
3. She is both industrious and a wise investor.
4. She is a good mother and her children are well taken care of.
5. She has a good reputation (Proverbs 31:10-31).

Your search Begins Here

Over the years many young men and women are challenged with discovering the right formula for finding a life partner. Some have someone in mind and are interested in confirming that the person is the will of God for them.

Others have a picture of their ideal spouse but don't know how to locate him or her. God has revealed to us the need to maintain the blood line which is not being unequally yoked. Strict adherence to the principles of maintaining the blood line should be the starting point of your search for a wife. Those that ignored this principle have often paid a heavy price for their disobedience.

When two unequal animals are yoked together, each animal has to work harder than necessary to till the soil or to transport goods. The animals have the added burden of managing the disparity in strength, height, weight and attitude.

The same is true of two individuals that have different beliefs. This is so critical that even the disparities in belief and maturity are bound to create problems during the marriage unless the couple works hard to bridge the disparity gap.

The main challenge of marrying outside your faith is the absence of a standard formula for problem solving. Problem solving involves making multiple decisions and taking steps that will lead to the solution. For couples that have the same belief, problem solving begins with prayers and following biblical principles.

Whether the challenge is health or finance the bible has already proffered solutions for those problems. Couples that have different belief systems have to decide whether to go to the hospital or prayer house, whether to get another job or go to church and pray, whether to pay their tithe or save their money. They experience crises of identity, loyalty, role models for the children, and confidence.

But Beyond the preservation of the blood line, the man searching should look to God to give him the desires of his heart.

Summary

1. God is interested in your marriage and wants you to maintain the spiritual blood line.
2. Determine your bloodline and stay within it.
3. Decide what is important to you and do not settle for less. You are better off waiting for the right person than marrying the first available suitor and suffering the consequences for the rest of your life.
4. The search for a wife should not be based on what is now but rather on what could be.
5. Be guided by Prophecy, Potentials and Prospect.

Together For Ever

Chapter 4

Modern Day Trends in Finding a Wife

Whether you adopt the Abraham method of preserving the blood line or follow the Jacob method of finding a companion from his blood line, the process of finding a wife is still a challenge. Today many platforms have evolved to aid the process. From Referral Agencies to Singles fellowship, the growing trend is providing more avenues for singles to meet, interact and hopefully find one another. These emerging platforms have their advantages and disadvantages.

1. Singles Ministry:

Singles ministry has evolved over the years as the most likely place for a Christian man or woman to find a spouse. The ministry provides available and ready singles the opportunity to network and interact closely with each other. The success of the singles ministry as a tool for finding your wife is that the members have a lot of areas of compatibilities in key areas of life such as: faith, money management, responsibilities of the spouses, communication, sex and romance. Other areas are as follows:

1. All members are presumed to share the same belief system,
2. Members are equally yoked or share the same blood line
3. Members have largely the same values in key areas of life
4. Membership is screened and controlled
5. The loyalty of the members is high
6. The values of the church are advanced
7. Membership is encouraged and fed from the parent church ensuring continuity and uniformity
8. The rules of engagement are clearly defined

The disadvantages of using the singles ministry in your church as an avenue for finding your wife are as follows:

1. You are limited to the pool of singles from your church. The bigger your church, the more singles you will have to choose from.

2. The members are sometimes too familiar with each to see them as potential spouse. The singles find it hard to imagine the transformation from a church member to husband/wife.

3. Familiarity may also make it difficult for the parties to properly assess prospects and potentials. The image of the young single man driving an old car for years while pursuing his education is hard to shed. The Single woman who sometimes came to church with ruddy hair may be too strong to forget.

4. Singles may be unduly influenced by inexperienced ministers in the Church in communicating the will of God for them. Some pastors have attempted to play the role of a match maker for their parishioners.

5. Not all the members are sincere about their faith. Those that are genuine are at varying levels of maturity. It is easy for wolfs in a sheep skin to join the church for the purpose of finding a "church girl" without the intention of continuing in the faith after the marriage.

Over all joining the singles' groups is the most effective way for a serious minded Christian to begin the process of finding a wife. Singles' ministry provides the resources for effective dating, courtship and also provides support for singles to maintain their chastity. Recently, Singles ministries have been networking with other similar ministries to increase the pool of singles to choose from. It gives the pastorate the opportunity to access the single person in the church and make appropriate recommendation to inquiring suitors.

2. Bachelors and Bachelorette Clubs:

We are seeing a new trend where eligible spinsters/bachelors organize themselves to facilitate interactions between the opposite sex ready and available for marriage. They accomplish this by hosting various social events like birthdays, open houses, Christmas parties and valentine parties exclusively for their members and their guests.

Even though membership is exclusive the individuals are mostly middle aged men and women from mixed backgrounds, high income earners, lawyers, doctors, and business people from different races, nationalities and faith. Research has shown that the effectiveness of such clubs in match making eligible couples is at the very most measured. These clubs lack the ingredients that the singles ministries enjoy. For instance there is no standard screening process for members. Members often cross boundaries by dating two or more members at the same time. Members do not share the same values and faith, and are not loyal to the club. It is not surprising that most have developed the reputation for hosting wild parties that defeat the very purpose for which they were established.

3. Referral Agencies

The super busy lifestyle of eligible bachelors and bachelorette and the wonders of internet networking have created both the problem and the solution for interaction of bachelors and spinsters from the convenience of their computers.

There are both professional match making agencies and dating agencies providing the services to expedite the process of finding a wife. Candidates register with match making agencies by providing their personal information and their desired match. The agencies collects data base of candidates and attempt to match candidates based on values, preferences, relationship goals, physical features and history. The professional agencies follow up with the candidates after the match is made and provide support and counseling.

The candidates are subjected to varying degrees of pre-screening before including them in their data base while some agencies simply provide the information and leave it to the candidates to choose who is compatible.

Critics of the match making agencies say the candidates leave much of the decision of who is a good wife in the hands of the agencies. Perhaps the problem of match making agencies is that it relies on the applicant's information. Reports from Reuters claim that as many as 30% of the candidates are married men and many of them lie about their age, weight, height and profession. While it is clear that such agencies succeed in providing the platform for many unions, it is unclear how long such unions last.

4. Pre-Arranged Marriage:

Pre-Arranged marriage is marriage arranged by someone other than the couple getting wedded. Pre-arranged marriage has been in existence all over the world and still prevalent in South East Asia and Africa. In the book of Genesis, Abraham sent his trusted servant to go and arrange for a wife for his only son Isaac.

In "marriage a-la-mode", the writer satirized the practice of pre-arranged marriage among the aristocrats of

Europe and highlighted the predictable disaster that often followed such arrangements. The main thing here is that the process is a family affair with the couples having little or no say in who they end up with. The families decide the compatibility of the couple and timing of the marriage. In some cultures the marriage may be arranged while the couple involved are still infants. The parents do this in anticipation of solemnizing the wedding when the couple reaches a certain age.

The marriage is used to advance the common interest of the families. Some marriages have been arranged to build alliances, maintain economic and social status, and to strengthen the bond of friendship. In recent times, marriages have been arranged between individuals from developed countries and third world countries for the purpose of obtaining immigration benefits. Parents from India and Pakistan are known to arrange marriages between American and European born children and the children of their relatives in India and Pakistan to help them emigrate to the United State or Europe.

Pre-arranged marriage should not be confused with forced marriage. Most pre-arranged marriages are done with the full consent and support of the couples. Forced marriage, is marriage arranged by someone other than the couple against the expressed wish of the couple wedding. In practice the line between pre-arranged marriage and forced marriage is often thin. Some arranged marriages become forced when the couple decide to cancel the wedding well into the preparation and pursuit of the wedding ceremony.

5. Mass Wedding:

Mass weddings have been made popular by the Rev. Moon of the Unification Church. People of similar beliefs, race and nationality gather at an agreed location and at specified time for the purpose of finding a wife or a husband. The unique thing here is that the meeting, the courtship, the engagement and marriage have to be completed during the meeting. And so, two completely different individuals arrive at the venue of the conference as single persons and leave a few days later married to the 'love of their weekend'.

Together For Ever

PART II

Before You get Married

Together For Ever

Chapter 5.

The Wonders of Premarital Counseling

The importance of premarital Counseling:

If marriage is one of the most important events in our lives, then premarital counseling sessions are some of the most important trainings in our life. Doctors study for several years to be licensed to practice medicine and prescribe treatment for people. A good number of doctors end up not practicing their trade and even those that do practice do so for only some years. For your counseling to be effective, you must not only desire counseling but understand the purpose of counseling and decide ahead of time what you want to get out of these sessions. Unfortunately many of us do not see the importance of premarital counseling.

Selecting the Right Counselor:

A man cannot give what he does not have. Two cannot work together except they agree? Your choice of marriage counselor must be carefully made based on your faith and the kind of marriage you desire to build. If you will not enroll in a school that is not accredited and does not offer the course you intend to take then you should not choose a counselor that is not qualified and does not offer the model of desired marriage.

In this day of internet, many submit the future of their marriage to some internet shrink that they hardly know. That reminds me of a man that invited his friend to mediate between him and his wife over a disagreement that they had, hoping that his friend will talk sense into his wife and stop her proposal for them to divorce. After listening to the couple, the friend advised that the best thing is for the couple to separate or divorce. The man's wife then said, "Well, even your friend thinks we should divorce." The couple separated and eventually divorced.

What then is premarital Counseling? Simply put this is the counseling before marriage. It is during premarital counseling that the couple prepares for the journey ahead, albeit a life long journey.

An effective premarital counseling should address the core issues of marriage including:

1. What is marriage?

Marriage has been described as a union of one male and one female into one. Adam described Eve as the bone of his bones and flesh of his flesh because she was taken out of him. He went ahead to name her Eve which means 'life'. Your spouse is literarily your life. There is no other relationship in the world with a greater bond, for a lifetime and more profound. You are expected to provide companionship for each other, provide sexual satisfaction for each other, procreate and pursue your destiny together. No other person will have greater impact on your destiny than your spouse.

A man once said that if he knew the significance of marriage and the finality of the choice of spouse, he would have given it a deeper thought than he did before marrying his wife. This may sound cruel and insensitive to his wife but it speaks of the irreplaceable nature of your choice of spouse. Marriage is one decision that God expects us to make once and only once in our lifetime. The scripture is very clear that God hates divorce! (Malachi 2:16).

Unfortunately most couples are motivated by other factors like love, beauty, material things, fame, family pressure, a sense of urgency etc. Every one of these factors will become insignificant before the end of your lifetime.

2. **What does marriage mean to each of the spouses?**

Although marriage is the union of one man and one woman, our idea of the functionality of marriage is largely derived from our experience. For most people marriage is whatever they saw mom and dad do in their households. Knowing where the couple is coming from will help them bring only the positive influences of their parents to their new home. It will also help the couple to be mindful of the baggage they are hauling from their background.

Women from households where the mother played a dominant role in family affairs will seek to play the same role. Men whose fathers were the bread winners and sole decision makers will seek to play such role too unless they make conscious effort to change. We know that women from polygamous homes tend to be more tolerant of their husbands concubines or girlfriends. Men whose fathers abused their mothers tend to be abusive of their wives, and women from abusive families are more likely to tolerate such behavior than others.

What kind of marriage do you desire? Make a conscious effort to work towards building it and walking away from your default marriage.

3. **Why do you want to get married?**

You will be surprised to hear the reasons people get married. Some of the reasons that we have heard over the years include, to have children, because I am getting old, to appease my parents and friends, for companionship, I need someone to take care of me because I am tired of working all my life etc.

If any of the spouses is getting married for the wrong reason that could affect the marriage later. For instance, if one spouse is getting married to have children, then the success of that marriage is dependent on the couple having at least one child. Conversely the marriage will fail if the couple has difficulty in having children.

Ask yourself, why am I getting married?

4. **Why do you want to marry her?**

Why this woman among all the women in the whole world? Why this woman of all the women in your life? Was she just lucky to be your last girl friend when you were ready to settle down? What is the most important goal that you want to accomplish by marrying this woman? What do you think she is bringing to the table of your new home?

The reasons that people have proffered for marrying their spouses range from the ordinary to the most bizarre:

a) **Love:** Is your love strong enough that you are willing to stake the rest of your live with this woman?

b) **Her physical beauty:** What happens when the physical beauty is gone?

c) **She looks like my mother:** Do you really want to live with your mother for the rest of your life?

d) **She is the opposite of your mother:** Surely there are some qualities of your mother that you cherish.

e) **She will make a good house wife, She cooks well, She is tall** etc

f) **She is from a wealthy family**? Are you willing to deal with the overreaching influence of her rich and famous family?

5. Why do you want to marry him?

The number one reason that women give for deciding to accept a marriage proposal is how nice and caring the man is to them. I always wonder what else the man is supposed to do other than show that he cares especially when he is trying to convince the woman to marry him. Research has shown that the most important need of the woman is security for her and her children.

Whether that security is expressed in the financial strength of a man or in the more traditional physical attributes like how tall, how eloquent or muscular the man, depends on the woman. And yet time and time again women say I do without considering the three "P"s of finding a man:

- **Potential:** Does this man possess the ability to provide a good home for you and your children? Is he focused, hardworking, discipline etc

- **Prospect:** Where is he now in the pursuit of those things that will provide security for you and your children? He has the brain to be a medical doctor but he is still in pre-med program at this time and you are ready for family.

- **Prophesy:** Have you personally confirmed that he is the will of God for you, or are you depending on what some other person heard or saw? Remember, it is your life. Adam was asleep when the Lord made his wife. Dial into your inner channel and locate your soul mate.

The question is whether love and affection alone are enough for you to commit the rest of your life to this man. What if he stops caring, or is unable to care?

6. What are your core values?

The couple needs to be aware of each other's core values. These are simply what the other party is not willing to part with. These core values are expressed in different ways including faith, family, career, goals in life etc. Any misunderstanding or lack of respect for these core values become problematic during the marriage.

In our 20 years of marriage ministry, no other core value has been more problematic than the lack of commitment to the relationship with God. Often a woman who grew up in the church, the daughter of an ordained Pastor marries a man that does not share her values or at the very least is unwilling to be totally devoted to God.

Because the relationship with God transcends all areas of our lives, the couple will be challenged in adopting principles of decision making, allocation of their resources and the proper way to raise the children. Ironically, it is the woman's relationship with God that attracted the man in the first place to this "well behaved, chaste, church going girl"

Another frequent core value area that is challenged is the area of career. The man wants a homemaker but marries a career minded woman and there begins the problem. This is a no win situation for the couple because whichever of the core values that the couple decides to pursue will leave one spouse with a life of regret and frustration.

It is recommended that the couple list their core values and agree during the courtship on how to accommodate each other. This must be done with all sense of objectivity and honesty. The couple should neither promise what they are not willing to offer, nor compromise what they are not willing to live without.

7. Premarital Counseling should highlight the Couple's differences?

Each couple should examine their background, history and identify the differences in upbringing and demeanor. Things as simple as celebrations/ holidays ought to be discussed and agreed on the best way to celebrate them. Some people grew up celebrating Christmas and Thanksgiving with the extended family while for some; the holiday period is a somber/sacred time to be celebrated in the solitude of their home with the nuclear family. This could be a problem if the parties fail to address it before the first holiday comes.

8. Focus on the expectations of the parties?

Apart from the core values, the couples need to discuss their individual expectations from the marriage. What kind of family do they want to establish and who plays what role? What is the place of the man and what is the place of the woman? If the woman desires to be taken care of and to be the home maker, this should be discussed. If the man wants his children to be home schooled by the woman which means that she will give up her career until the children get to a certain age, this should be discussed and agreed upon. The role of the extended families in the nuclear family and interaction with third parties should also be discussed.

9. It is a time to prepare for effective courtship?

Finally, premarital counseling prepares the couple for effective courtship by providing the agenda for the courtship and pointing out areas for disclosure and discussions. The counselor also draws the couple's attention to the boundaries that God has set for Courtship. It is easy for couples who have set a date for marriage, perhaps obtained a marriage license to assume that they are married. Nothing is further from the truth because they are not yet married. Premarital Counseling is a time for the couple to ask questions about the marriage relationship.

Together For Ever

Chapter 6

The Wonders of Effective Courtship

Courtship is the period before engagement or marriage. It is the act, period, or art of seeking the love of someone with the intent to marry. It can be likened to the period in negotiation, when a letter of intent is exchanged between the parties without any obligation on the parties to deal except a promise to explore the possibility of marriage. It is at best an expression of intention. The success of the courtship period depends on the disclosures that are made by the couple and the objectivity of the assessment.

One of the challenges of courtship is the management of emotions that are stirred up by mental closeness of the parties and the thought of the possibility of marriage. Couples must strive to honor God, themselves and their parents. It is important that the couple is not coerced into making commitment to marry because they have already engaged in premarital sex. The number one goal during courtship must be to protect each other from sexual sin. Sexual sin should be avoided at all costs because it creates distrust, guilt and shame.

Unfortunately the period of courtship is the most likely period for premarital sex to occur because courtship is the simulation of marriage relationship without sexual intercourse.

Some organizations and counselors recommend some dos and don'ts designed to help the couple to deal with this pressure packed period of high testosterone and poetry. Each couple must establish parameters and be aware of their strengths and weaknesses. It is important to have an open discussion about it before setting boundaries.

Only God knows how many couples cross this boundary during this period. For a friend of mine who is a Christian brother, the cat was let out of the bag because the wife gave birth before the ninth month of their wedding and the baby was not premature. You may argue that a child born in the eight month could be born healthy and to that I say true, only God can tell.

It is difficult to recommend rules for courtship because no two couples are the same but there are some general dos and don'ts.

1. Avoid being alone in a private place.
2. Intersperse your programs with a lot of spiritual exercises, i.e. bible studies and praying and fasting.
3. Discuss your boundaries ahead of time and be honest about it
4. Avoid using pet names like 'Honey' and 'Dear'.

5. Absolutely no sleep over in each other's apartment or house or late night visits.
6. Avoid watching suggestive movies together especially in a private place.
7. Find other courting Christian couples and plan outings together.
8. Find a mentor that you are comfortable with and accountable to.
9. Constantly remind yourselves that you are not yet married.
10. Be ready to cancel program or activities that you cannot handle.
11. Absolutely no phone sex or sex-texting
12. Above all, pray for one each other.

Together For Ever

Chapter 7

Group Association/Peer Bonding.

A Peer group is a social group of individuals that share a common interest. Any misalignment in the commonality of interest will make the group ineffective. If you have a peer group consisting of newlywed couples closely related in age, years in marriage, social class but with different views of marriage, such a group will be dysfunctional.

This goal may be short term or for life. A good example of a peer group is the alcoholic anonymous (AA). The role of peer groups in marriage is to exchange information and provide support to members for dealing with common problems that couples face. Peer groups provide unique context for cognitive, social and emotional growth in marriage (Internet definition for Peer group).

There are both formal and informal peer groups. Informal peer groups are groups comprising mainly of friends, class mates, co workers etc. Although the informal peer groups usually have few members, such groups are highly effective in influencing the growth of the marriage of the members.

At the beginning of our marriage we were blessed to be a part of small peer group that evolved from friendship. Although the core members of the peer were only three couples, the group welcomed other couples to join and leave on their own terms.

We had a lot in common as we had all started our families, got married the same year, graduated from college about the same time and migrated to the United States over the same period of time. We had known ourselves even before our weddings and shared the same faith. We were all within the same age range. We met frequently especially during the major holidays to celebrate and encourage one other. Today all three couples are established in marriage.

The formal peer groups are those established by organizations and institutions such as colleges, nonprofit organizations, churches and companies. Some of such peer groups meet periodically to discuss marital concerns and seek out solutions based on the principles in the bible. Couples married within a time range are grouped together and assigned a meeting venue, time of meeting, facilitators and the curriculum. Although the group is also evangelistic, the primary focus is to provide support for the members.

Chapter 8

Role of Models and Mentors

Mentoring in marriage relationships is a trusting and collaborative process in which the parties commit their time to series of interactions for the betterment of their marriage.

In this sense the mentor is usually one that has acquired more experience, skill, knowledge and/or higher position than the mentee (protégé). There is an African proverb that says that what a young man can't see while standing up, an old man has already seen while sitting down.

Mentoring may be formal or informal. Whether the agreement to mentor and be mentored is in writing or not, the objectives and the expectations of the parties must be clearly expressed. Other essential rules of engagement must be understood, like frequency of meeting, the location of meeting, confidentiality, involvement of spouses, and what to do if the relationship is not working for either of the parties.

All marriages gravitate toward what the couples observed from their homes while growing up. Our parents or guardians are invariably our first mentors in the area of marriage. Therefore, without effective premarital counseling, couples tend to start their marriage lives with different orientations of what marriage is and what it should be. Joint mentoring program alleviates some of the potential areas of conflict as a result of the orientations.

Choosing a Mentor.

It is very important to choose your mentor very carefully. Remember the mentor is transferring life altering information to you and you are very vulnerable to his or her undue influence. The search for a mentor begins with deciding what kind of marriage you desire and then locating mentors that exemplify the ideals.

Conduct your own research by asking questions, interviewing the couples, meeting with the prospective mentor couple before even asking to be mentored. You may consider having multiple mentors for different areas of your marriage or life. For instance you may choose a mentor for balancing marriage and carrier and another for child rearing.

A good mentor must be;

1. a good listener and a strategist;
2. has valuable knowledge and teaching skills;
3. must be a role model;
4. challenge and affirm the mentee and;

5. must be very accessible to the mentee and
6. committed to the success of the mentee;

Marriage mentors play essential roles by offering viable alternatives for living as husband and wife in the following areas:

1. There is need for acquisition of expertise, experience and knowledge for maintaining the purity and originality of the marriage institution.

2. New couples need to acquire essential competencies to better manage their homes and relationships, especially in the areas in customs, culture, language, communication, money management, sex and child rearing.

3. In this ever changing world new couples are offered alternative lifestyles and experimentation that makes it difficult to decide which option is better for the new couples

Marriage mentoring offer tremendous mutual benefits to the protégés as follows:

1. Acceleration of learning and acquisition of competencies. This insures stability and rapid maturity of the couples.

2. Mentors offer guidance and resources in time of difficulty often drawing from their wealth of knowledge and experience.

3. Mentors strengthen the bond between husbands and wives by acting as a positive sounding board.

4. Mentors offer continuing education, orientation and training to the couples in all areas of their life and at any stage. From the beginning to the college days.

PART III

Now That You Are Married

Together For Ever

Chapter 9

The Four Phases of a Marriage Relationship

Every relationship evolves through four phases of place and time. The four Phases are as follows:

1. the Phase of the Romance,
2. the Phase of Reality,
3. the Phase of Rethinking and
4. the Phase of Recommitment/Renunciation

These phases of the relationships are inter-connected without any noticeable line of demarcation. What you do in one phase affects the other phases. Relationship is subject to the natural law of seed.

The quality and quantity of the seed you sow in one phase of time and place determines your harvest in the preceding phase. From the time of finding your wife through the wedding and living together happily ever after, the relationship passes through phases of time and place.

Having a good understanding of the phases and making sound preparation for the next phase determines whether your marriage will be made in heaven or earth.

1. **The Phase of the Romance:** The Phase of Idealism.

Romance and love have been known to start in both the beautiful and bizarre of places. People have found love in prisons and palaces, at their points of death and place of birth. For some it is love at first sight and for others, the sudden realization that their best friend is now the love of their life. Such is the power of love.

Once romance starts, the behavior trail is the same; excitement,
extreme indifference to reality, excessive investment of time and energy
in self discovery, celebrating their similarities and honoring their difference.

At this phase, nothing matters but the sight of each other. To give legitimacy to the relationship, the couple invoke the "C" word; Courtship. Like king Solomon the "beloved's eyes is like doves and her lips are like scarlet ribbon".

I remember this phase of my life in college. I had met my wife December 1983 just as we were about to go on Christmas holidays. I can tell you that I spent that holiday day dreaming. My wife and I spent inordinate amount of time talking about ourselves and planning our lives. We were going to have the biggest law office ever, build a mansion with an ivory floor, cream colored couches and travel the world. We dreamt and fantasized all day long. We never courted in the true sense of it.

Efficient management of the phase of romance will involve realistic appraisal of the strengths and weaknesses of each of the parties. Accurate assessment of each other is the beginning of successful marriage. Objective discussion of these areas of incompatibility is crucial to soft landing and cruising through the reality phase. Such discussion should proceed as follows:

1. Make a list of the areas of incompatibilities and differences between you and your spouse. You can do this by having each other make a list and later comparing notes. After that arrange the master list according to your level of tolerance and importance. Be realistic in identifying these differences.

2. Discuss these areas of differences with your partner and agree on which of the differences are strengths and which ones are weaknesses. Talk about the advantages of the differences and the disadvantages. For instance, an insecure man is most likely a family oriented man and a faithful lover.

   Decide on the areas of differences that you cannot live with and agree on what to do. Exchange commitment with each other on how to handle the differences. Anger management or drinking problem can be resolved through joint counseling. If the woman is independent because of long period of being a spinster, marriage counseling and better understanding will help.

3. Be sure that you are prepared to live with the differences for the rest of your life especially in the core areas of your relationship. Don't assume that your spouse will change from being easy going to serious minded later, indoor man to outgoing man. Or more seriously from being insecure to a super confident man. At the very least be prepared to live with it until he changes or learn to celebrate your differences.

The closer you are in simulating reality at this phase will prepare you for a smoother transition to the next phase and also help you escape the shocking ordeal of the next phase.

2. **The Phase of Reality:** This is the Phase of Ordeal-ism.

Unlike the phase of romance, the reality phase comes unexpectedly. You are still basking in the sun of your romance and then you realize that the honeymoon is over and you have to go to work now. The very things that were fun start being frustrating. All the details that were left out of the ideal world during the phase of romance come seeking for attention.

Couples find out that their ideal world of romance is far from reality. New discoveries of differences or incompatibilities are not welcomed or accommodated. Some feelings of disappointment and deceit creep into the mind. Misunderstandings become disagreements. Time to deploy the most advanced Dispute Resolution System in your arsenal. This is capable of becoming both cold war and world war if the parties have no system for dispute resolution. Even a well designed Dispute Resolution System will be challenged as the parties learn to give and take.

To make matters worse, the woman is likely to discover that she is pregnant, (again a casualty of the excessive indulgence in the romance phase). As she undergoes the hormonal changes in her body she becomes withdrawn and difficult to please. The man is confused, suspicious and impatient. Pregnancy and child birth interfere with the quality of time that the couple enjoys together. Money and allocation of the couple's resources is magnified. The woman thinks about saving and security while the man wants to take risk and taste the waters.

The woman is often unromantic at this time with sex becoming routine. The man reeling from the overdose of the preceding phase feels abandoned. Poor and immature language skills make communication difficult and ineffective.

The Man reverts to hanging out with his old buddies to escape the lack of excitement and nagging at home. Now the woman feels abandoned and nags more about everything else but the real issues.

Couples are initially embarrassed to talk about these challenges with each other. Some women complain to their confidants, mothers, best friends, ex-boyfriends, co workers, pastors etc. The rate of infidelity and divorce is high during the first 2 years of marriage.

For couples that managed their romance phase well, the reality phase is challenging but not nearly as much as those that just had fun during the proceeding phase. Whatever the situation, here are a few primers on what to do:
1. Understand that what you are going through is normal and that it is not peculiar to you.
2. Review your list of differences during your romance phase.
3. Talk to your pastor, marriage counselor or mentor.
4. Avoid talking to your mom, dad, ex-boyfriend or girlfriend about what you are going through.
5. Make a commitment not to say anything bad about your spouse.
6. Join a marriage support group and invest in learning more about your marriage.
7. Don't ever quit.

3. The Phase of Rethinking:

"But Jesus said to him, "No one, having put his hand to the plow, and looking back, is fit for the kingdom of God" (Luke 9:62).

The feeling of frustration, disappointment and loneliness during the reality phase eventually gives way to critical thinking and solution seeking. Couples begin to review their assumptions and expectations alone. They compare promises and assertions made during the courtship phase.

Your ideal spouse begins to look like an ordeal spouse. What seemed just right and perfect suddenly looks bad and imperfect. Suddenly the offers for marriage that you rejected begin to look like missed opportunities. At this time the parties are very vulnerable to indoctrination and infidelity.

For most couples there are three Options:

>**The Status Quo Option:** You accept the way things are and focus on other things that interest you. Some focus on their career, children or home making while tolerating each other. Communication breaks down completely because of lack of trust. It sometimes degenerates into verbal abuse/ physical attacks because of a feeling of deceit. Intimacy between the couple is non-existent or mechanical. Some couples stop sharing their matrimonial bed. The man sleeps on the couch or moves to the guest room. One in every ten marriages live together by tolerating each other.

The Divorce/Separation Option: Five in every ten marriages throw in the towel within the first five years of their marriage. Couples decide that they have made their choice based on false assumptions. Some rationalize that they have either fallen out of love or were never in love from the beginning.

Breakdown in communication leads to lack of intimacy and loneliness. Emotional separation leads to physical separation and finally legal separation. The filing of divorce or consulting a lawyer to file a divorce is the nail on the coffin of a dead union. No one files divorce in a happy marriage.

For some couples everything is perfectly well except for the lack of excitement of the romance phase. That reminds me of the story of a couple that divorced because of lack of excitement. The woman testified that the man was a wonderful man, hard worker and a great dad to their children. During their courtship and at the beginning of the marriage they were inseparable and she looked forward to the end of the day when they both returned home from the day's work. Then she lost interest and could not feel the excitement anymore. Asked if there was a third party or outside interest she swore there was none at the time.

First she tried to shake off the feeling by pretending that she was excited. Soon her husband started complaining and she began to feel guilty and sorry for her husband. Finally, she told her husband that she believes that he deserved better. She was filling for divorce to give him the opportunity to move on and find someone better. Both parties got divorced but stayed close for many years working together to raise their children. Today the woman regrets the decision and still wonders what happened to her. She is still single but he got married a few years ago after many years of living alone.

Adjustment and continuation option: This is the rethinking option that objectively reviews the assumptions and expectations against the backdrop of what is real and available. You thought you married a very careful man, always taking his time to make the right decision but now you see a man who has difficulty making up his mind. You wanted a woman who will keep the house but now her clothes are all over the room and none in the closet. Instead of questioning your initial assumptions, objectively review and analyze it for areas of adjustment. That adjustment process starts with your decision to stay married and continues with investment in resources that will help your marriage including counseling and attending marriage seminars.

4. **The Phase of Recommitment:**

This is the phase of wisdom and applied knowledge. At this stage you begin to invest in your marriage and find solutions to your challenges. The principles of Ephesians 5: 23-33 become practical and real. Husbands, love your wives, just as Christ also loved the church and paid the ultimate price for her. Wives, submit to your own husbands as unto the Lord. Recognize that your obedience to the plan of God in marriage and your willingness to play your assigned roles faithfully is a service to God.

Chapter 10

The Art of Staying Married

One of the greatest mysteries of life is the making of two completely different persons with different backgrounds, learning, expectations etc into one pursuing the same goal. The bible recognizes that the two shall become one. The word "shall" implies that oneness in marriage is a process and not an automated event.

The exchange of vows, the kissing of the bride, the witnesses and the entire marriage ceremony is the beginning of a life long journey to oneness. Many assume that exchange of vows is the beginning and end of the process of uniting two bodies, two souls and two spirits into one. But Oneness in Marriage can only be achieved through the conscious effort of both the husband and wife to be one.

The blessing of marriage is reserved for those who give up their individuality to become one and remain one. It is at this altar of oneness and singleness of heart that the man becomes fruitful and multiplies, and the woman becomes the helper of destiny. Oneness breeds synchronicity without frictions with undivided attention to the destiny of the couple.

"Behold how good and how pleasant it is for brethren to dwell together in unity! It is like the precious oil upon the head, running down on the beard, The beard if Aaron, Running down on the edge of his garments. It is like the dew of Hermon, Descending upon the mountains of Zion; For there the Lord commanded the blessing – Life forevermore" (Psalm 133:1-3).

God has prepared a special blessing for your household that is only available when you become one and work together in unity. The couple that cannot work together will not partake of the blessing because they will never get to the dinner table. Why is it so important that husband and wife work together?

"Two *are* better than one, Because they have a good reward for their labor. For if they fall, one will lift up his companion. But woe to him *who is* alone when he falls, For *he has* no one to help him up. Again, if two lie down together, they will keep warm; But how can one be warm alone? Though one may be overpowered by another, two can withstand him. And a threefold cord is not quickly broken" (Ecclesiastes 4:9-12).

The first benefit of husband and wife working together is economics. The reward of their effort is better than one person working alone or two persons working individually.

The second benefit is risk management and security. If either spouse falls short in their endeavors, the other will lift him up. In other words, one spouse is a security and protector of the other spouse should he fall. The net effort of this is that the couples that work together take confident risk knowing the other spouse got their back. While the couple that work alone are less confident in taking bold steps.

Anyone who has nobody to help him up when he falls is cursed because he is likely to remain in a fallen state from the fall.

The third benefit of working together is companionship and support during trials and tribulations of life. The loneliest time for singles and couples that do not work together is during trials. Sicknesses, failed businesses, bad investments, accidents est. incapacitate the most agile of human beings.

I know a person who was divorced from his wife, he found himself alone in a foreign land after a near fatal accident. The doctors had given him forty eight hours to live but he made it only to wish he had died. Why because he was lonely and felt abandoned by the world. But God touched his ex-wife's heart to care for him and nurse him back into life. Without the ex-wife's support and encouragement, he would not have had any reason to continue living.

When all is well, the need for a companion is hardly noticed.

Couples that work together provide joint protection and security for themselves against falling flat on their faces. Couples can overcome trials and challenges that can easily overwhelm either of them. I know a man who lost his license to practice his trade for a period of six months. The man was advised by other professionals to close his office, fire his staff, disconnect his phone services and go home for six months. For most professionals that misfortune would have crippled and decimated them. But this man kept his office open, paid for the utilities and maintained the status quo because his wife took extra shifts at her job, kept encouraging the man until his license was restored. The office stayed open, utilities remained active without the need to terminate any of the services. The man fell down but was lifted up by his companion. The enemy desired to truncate the man's destiny but the wife protected him from shame and destruction.

Finally, true union of husband and wife includes the Holy Spirit. God is the third strand in the cord that is not quickly torn apart. Couples that are not one cannot attract the presence of God in their lives. They lack the divine protection of the Lord. the man's prayers are hindered, and they lose the benefit of the presence of God in their gathering because they are not one.

Chapter 11

Communication Skills That Work in Marriage

"He who guards his mouth preserves his life, But he who opens wide his lips shall have destruction" (Proverbs 13:3).

Communication is the strongest cord that holds marriages together. The ability to communicate our deepest thoughts and feelings in a manner that is clearly understood and accepted is an invaluable skill that rises to the level of an art and should be coveted by every spouse desiring to build a long lasting relationship.

Your marriage will rise or fall with the effectiveness of your communication skills. God made it so and the devil knows it too.

We read the story of a group of men who set out on a grand project of constructing a tower high enough to reach Heaven. The motive was to make a name for themselves and to prevent their generation from dispersing around earth contrary to the instruction of their maker for them to be fruitful and multiply. The men were unstoppable in the pursuit of their project.

> The Lord said, "Indeed the people are one and they all have one language, and this is what they begin to do; now nothing that they propose to do will be withheld from them" (Genesis 11:6).

The success of the project depended on the two indispensible factors of effective teamwork and partnership:

> **Unity of purpose:** The men had the same goal of making a name for themselves and staying together.
>
> **Unity of Language**: Language skills gave them the ability to maintain the unity of purpose. Can you imagine the brick layer asking for brick and getting water, or the foreman calling for a lunch break as the workers continue to work.

When spouses consummate their marriage they become one with each other and that oneness is irrevocable. No power can reverse a covenant that is sealed with the exchange of blood. The most delicate soft target in your marriage is your marital language and that is why it is a battle ground in the spirit realm.

Notice that "Nothing which they purpose to do will be impossible". Can you imagine God saying this about you and your spouse? The power of speaking the same language is so potent that God could only intervene by changing the language of the men. Every problem in the marriage is a problem of communication.

> "Come let us go down and there confuse their language, that they may not understand one another's speech.
>
> So the Lord scattered them abroad from there over the ace of all the earth, and they ceased building the city". (Genesis 11:7,8)

Communication occurs when there is a meeting of the mind between two or more persons. Two cannot work together except they agree!

The same principle is true of several marriages. At the beginning of each relationship couples communicate more and enjoy the relationship better. One statistics shows that couples communicate with each other for an average of 4-5 hours a day during the period of courtship and dating, but only five minutes after marriage. One woman told me recently that in a whole day, the only communication she had with her husband for the whole day was "I need the blanket".

The high level of communication between new couples at the beginning of the marriage helps them to pursue their projects more efficiently. The project of engagement, wedding, honey moon and settling down are carried out with ease because of the oneness between the parties. Unfortunately the languages change soon after and confusion set in. No wonder the unions begin to disintegrate just like the men building the tower of Babel did. This is not the will of God for marriage.

Elements of Effective Communication:

> "A soft answer turns away wrath, But a harsh word stirs up anger. The tongue of the wise uses knowledge rightly but the mouth of fools pours forth foolishness" (Proverbs 15:1,2).

Effective communication in marriage requires disciplined attention to little details like the eye contact, the posture of the body, the tone of the voice, feedbacks and much more. The art of communication is a total package of the observation of these intricate parts and the accurate interpretation of their meaning.

The effective communicator focuses his attention on the audience, uses the right tone and body posture to transfer information. Often times the tone of our voice conveys our negative emotion of anger, fear, distrust, hate while our words are soothing. This is very evident when an apology is coerced from an unrepentant spouse. One spouse says "I am sorry" and the other spouse immediately retorts, "No you are not" or "You don't mean it".

Effective communication requires two foundational skills:

Listening Skill:

It is said that the most important element of communication is listening attentively to the communicator. Listening involves a lot of discipline that many of us lack. Research has shown that we hear only about 50% of what is being communicated to us. That number is very generous in marriage because there is more selective hearing in marriage.

God gave everyone of us two ears and one mouth. Perhaps he was trying to tell us something when he said "swift to hear and slow to speak". And as is always the case we are not listening. We are often in a hurry to be heard than to hear others speak.

Listening requires total attention to the communicator's verbal and non verbal languages. Research has shown that conversation is divided into the following:

I. Your words only convey 7% of what you are saying
II. The tone of your voice represents 38% of what's on your mind;
III. Your body language communicates 55% of your mind.

Effective listening means active participation in the conversation. As Joe Girard put it:

"Smile when the other person smiles, frown in agreement if he frowns. Use facial expressions that show you are listening. Believe me it will be appreciated". (**How to Sell yourself).**

Seven Keys to horn your listening skills:

1. Seek to understand before you start preparing for your response. After all your position may not be different from what you are hearing and if so what is the point repeating the position. Listen with your mouth closed it opens your ears wider and deeper.

2. Listen with all your faculties. Your posture, your eyes, your facial expression est. must be focused on the conversation for you to hear more than the average 50% result.

3. Focus on the speaker. Avoid interruptions. It is distracting the speaker.

4. Speak only when you have the other person's undivided attention and only after you have understood the communication.

5. Seek to clarify positions and information passed on during the conversation.

6. Listen to all the communication tools of the speaker. The eyes, the body, the tone etc.

7. Constantly remind yourself that the essence of speaking is to pass along some information. If your information is stale or redundant, you may want to keep it to yourself.

The Ability to determine the right Time and Place:

While listening is the most important element of communication, the effective communicator has the added obligation of choosing the right time and the right place to introduce a subject matter in their communication. The person initiating the communication must decide the appropriateness of the time and the place. Sometimes the suitability of a time is obvious and sometimes it is not. It may be unsuitable for the wife to initiate conversation about serious monetary issues while the husband is watching championship football. Conversely it may be unsuitable for a man to initiate a discussion about sex when his wife is sleepy, irritated and/or tired.

The Purpose of Communication in Marriage:

The lips of the wise disperse knowledge (Proverbs 15:7a).

There are four main purposes for communication. You must be clear on your objective before you initiate each communication. Your purpose in communicating will determine your choice of approach.

1. **To exchange information**: The primary purpose of communication is to exchange information consisting of thoughts, feelings, facts, and fictions. Couples that communicate less with each other know little about each other and respond the least to the needs of their spouses.

Couples that communicate several times during the day provide situational report of occurrences in their lives and continue the discussion when they get back home. It is essential that both parties have the same information. Studies have shown that couples that communicate frequently transfer their language skills to each other including their choice of vocabulary and the communication mannerism as time goes.

Such couple also share wealth of information together both professional information and ordinary information. In so doing they develop a marriage language exclusively for themselves.

2. **Conflict Resolution**: Communication is essential for resolving differences in the family and clarifying individual positions. Couples that have effective communication channels and skills resolve their differences faster and with finality than couples that do not communicate with each other on a regular basis. When there is no mechanism for stating and clarifying positions, minor differences become major disagreements. As the days go by facts become fussy and distorted according to individual perceptions. Each spouse restates and interprets what he/she believes he/she heard according his/her own understanding.

3. **Communication helps growth and Maturity in faith**: Our mouths speak from the preoccupations of our heart. Couples who frequently communicate with each other encourage one another in the Christian race. The subject matter of the communication between couples often revolves

around on-the-spot events or matters that interest both spouses.

For Christian couples the subject matter invariably revolves around lessons learned from bible studies, church, testimonials and temptations. Biblical principles are restated, reviewed and applied during the conversation and real life challenges are addressed from scriptural solutions. It is not unusual for couples to discuss incidents at work including improper advances from the opposite sex, maltreatment of co-workers and superiors.

4. Personal Growth of the Spouses: Communication enhances our self control and self discipline in all aspects of our life. Through frequent communication we horn the skill of expressing our feelings, emotions, and thoughts in an honest and objective manner. We also learn the discipline of listening, understanding, tolerating and accommodating one another.

At the beginning of every relationship, couples invest much more in communicating their feelings more than facts. As the years go by the communication become largely information exchange as the couple's marital language increases.

Together For Ever

Chapter 12

Sex is God's Idea

If communication is the engine that powers the relationship between husband and wife, sex is the oil that lubricates it. Better romance and sexual relationship reduces conflict between husband and wife. Without satisfying sex the engine of the relationship runs rough, the body runs slow and ultimately grinds to a halt. Such is the paralyzing power of sex.

Sex has both spiritual significance and physical value. A marriage union is signed and sealed but not delivered until it is consummated by the couple. Any marriage that is not consummated is legally voidable and can be annulled as if it never existed.

I know this might shock some people but it's a fact and it's the truth, that Sex is God's idea not man's idea. He designed and invented it. And if it's God's idea, then it is a very good idea. Man did not invent nor design sex, God did from the very beginning. It was not an afterthought, He had it in mind all along even before the creation and that is why He created the sexual organs in the first place. And when the creation was completed, it was one of the first charges that God gave man.

Sex is an important part of the marriage relationship invented, designed and formulated by our Maker and it's nothing for anyone to be ashamed of, but to have ultimate pleasure in it.

I hereby submit to you therefore that there is nothing dirty or unclean about the sexual relationship between a man and his wife; it is as clean as having a church fellowship in fact there is no greater fellowship than a man and his wife having sexual intercourse.

God is pleased with this because you are using the organs He made for the exact purpose for which He made them and you are therefore fulfilling a divine purpose. A marriage relationship in which there is no sexual relationship, except for medical or physiological reasons, is not fulfilling the purpose of God.

When God made Adam and Eve, He gave them charge to: "Prosper! Reproduce! Fill Earth! Take charge! Be responsible for fish in the sea and birds in the air, for every living thing that moves on the face of Earth" (Genesis 1:28 The Message). So we see God's first instruction to Adam and Eve to Reproduce! For there to be reproduction, there has to be coupling…sex.

And again, the bible states that, "Therefore a man shall leave his father and mother and be joined to his wife, and they shall become one flesh. And they were both naked, the man and his wife, and were not ashamed" (Genesis 2:24,25).

Becoming one flesh also connotes that there will actually be a physical intimate relationship between a man and his wife. Such that when this happens there will be nakedness and no shame or disgust will be felt by any of the parties, rather it will be one of acceptance and pleasure for both sides.

I need to point out at this point that God's idea of sex is that this act will be enjoyed by both husband and wife **ONLY.** In order words, where husband is a man and wife is a woman. It is a gift a man gives to his wife and vice versa.

Apostle Paul states that, "Now, getting down to the questions you asked in your letter to me. First, Is it a good thing to have sexual relations? Certainly- but only within a certain context. It's good for a man to have a wife, and for a woman to have a husband. Sexual drives are strong, but marriage is strong enough to contain them and provide for a balanced and fulfilling sexual life in a world of sexual disorder. (I Corinthians 7:1,2 The Message).

The marriage bed must remain honorable at all times. "Marriage *is* honorable among all, and the bed undefiled; but fornicators and adulterers God will judge" (Hebrews 13:4). God is against a married man or woman defiling the marriage bed at any given time either by adultery or fornication.

He made sex to be enjoyed by the man and his wife, which did not include a third party. Man has dictated to the world what sex should be. But unfortunately this is not the idea of God and as such God Himself frowns at and judges illicit sex.

"There's more to sex than mere skin on skin. Sex is as much a spiritual mystery as it is physical fact. As written in Scripture, "The two become one" (I Corinthians 6:16 The Message).

Sex as God's idea goes beyond the physical. It is a soulish experience as well as spiritual. God never intended sexual intercourse to be a free for all act. God detests free for all sex. Sex as God intended it is for pleasure and reproduction between a husband and his wife.

Sexual acts before marriage is termed fornication while the same acts with a third party after marriage is termed adultery. God hates both fornication and adultery. The marriage bed must not be defiled by either of this. He made this clear through Apostle Paul in Hebrews 13:4 "Honor marriage, and guard the sacredness of sexual intimacy between wife and husband. **God draws a firm line against casual and illicit sex**" (The Message).

We live in the world where sex is everything…in fact sex sells. If you are involved in any entertainment and sex is not embedded in it, it will not be attractive to the public. The public may be attracted alright but the question is, "Is God attracted by it?" No! Instead God draws a firm line against casual and illicit sex.

What about sexual promiscuity? God frowns seriously against this and He takes firm stand against it too. God, through Apostle Paul, again cautions, "We must not be sexually promiscuous - they paid for that, remember, with twenty-three thousand (23,000) deaths in one day!" (I Corinthians. 10:8 The Message). Folks this is serious! Twenty three thousand people dropping dead in one day because of this stuff? It's time to begin to take this a lot more seriously. In our days we have seen so many lives claimed by sexually transmitted diseases than ever before.

The reason why there is such a grave consequence on illicit and casual sex is because sex is not just mere skin on skin relationship, it goes way beyond that. You are joined together in soul and spirit with whoever you have sex with. If you have sex with your spouse you are joined as one, which is God's design, but If you have sex with a harlot the bible says, you are one with her also.

"There is a sense in which sexual sins are different from all others. In sexual sin we violate the sacredness of our own bodies, these bodies were made for God-given and God-modeled love, for "becoming one" with another" (1 Corinthians. 6:18 The Message).

THE PURPOSE OF SEX

If sex is God's idea what then is the purpose of the sexual relationship between a man and his wife. Why did God make sex? What did He have in mind? Why is it such a big deal? These are some of the questions we need to attempt to develop in this book.

1. Sealing the covenant

Marriage is a covenant not a contract. Every covenant has a seal. The marriage covenant is not exempt from this. The sexual relationship between a man and his wife is the celebration of that seal of the marriage covenant. In the time of old, covenant is not binding until it is sealed with blood. Well that is what we see in the marriage covenant.

Sexual union provided for the seal with blood in that for those who are virgins, blood is shed, thereby sealing that covenant. This is God's intention! It is that in a marriage covenant, with the seal of sexual union, that husband and wife will be one and will be joined together and become one flesh; and this union so sacred and so exclusive, that it must not be desiccated by anyone.

However if you are unmarried and reading this book and you are not a virgin, you are not condemned. The blood of Jesus cleanses you from all sins if you have asked for forgiveness and makes all things new for you.

"Therefore, if anyone *is* in Christ, *he is* a new creation; old things have passed away; behold, all things have become new" (2 Corinthians 5:17). For as the scriptures have said,

"*There is* therefore now no condemnation to those who are in Christ Jesus, who do not walk according to the flesh, but according to the Spirit" (Romans 8:1).

2. Procreation

One of the primary purposes of the sexual relationship between a man and his wife is that of procreation. God commanded Adam and Eve to be fruitful and to multiply, to reproduce after their kind. So we see that sexual union is a channel where by multiplication is achieved here on earth. It takes coupling together in a sexual union for children to be brought forth. That was exactly what Adam and Eve did.

"Now Adam knew Eve his wife, and she conceived and bore Cain, and said, I have acquired a man from the Lord." (Genesis 4:1). "Behold, children *are* a heritage from the Lord, The fruit of the womb *is* a reward. Like arrows in the hand of a warrior, So *are* the children of one's youth. Happy *is* the man who has his quiver full of them; They shall not be ashamed, But shall speak with their enemies in the gate." (Psalm 127:3-5).

3. Pleasure

"Let your fountain be blessed, And rejoice with the wife of your youth. *As a* loving deer and a graceful doe, Let her breasts satisfy you at **all times**; And always be **enraptured** with her love" (Proverbs 5:18-19).

The word enraptured means to be literally intoxicated with her love that is pleasure. Sexual intimacy was designed by God to give a man and his wife the highest form of sensual pleasure. The whole of the book of Songs of Solomon is dedicated to the celebration of love between a man and his wife.

The pleasure of the sexual relation in a marriage union was so paramount in God's agenda that He moved Moses to instruct the people of Israel that when one gets married, he needs to take off for a whole year from fighting wars so he can stay home and give himself and his wife pleasure.

"When a man has taken a new wife, he shall not go out to war or be charged with any business; he shall be free at home one year, and bring happiness to his wife whom he has taken" (Deuteronomy 24:5).

Unfortunately married couples have robbed themselves of this pleasure we are talking about and have relegated their relationship to business as usual where there is no fun, no sizzle and therefore no pleasure in their marriage.

On the other hand some people have perverted the sexual union between man and woman with all kinds of inappropriate ways to enter into this sexual union. Most married couples have thrown in the towel in this area and are continually making a shipwreck of their marriage relationship.

It is time to rise and begin enjoying the pleasure that God has designed for your marriage. Statistically, the couples that enjoy and have pleasurable sexual relationship with each other make the happiest homes and affair proof their marriages.

4. Recreation

Sex and intimacy can be the best sport a man can ever play with his wife. It can be compared to tennis, or golf. The same way you train for this other sports is the same way you train for sex and intimacy. On the other hand the same benefit you receive from these sports is the same benefit you receive from sex and intimacy.

For those couples who have sexual relationships very infrequently, you will soon be out of shape like you would be if you don't engage in other sporting activities. No one ever made it to the Hall of Fame by remaining stagnant. Learning something new will keep you and your partner on your toes. Nothing's worse than running the same play over and over, especially when it doesn't always work. So, learn some new moves and enjoy.

Isaac caught this vision and decided that even though he found himself in a foreign land, in the presence of famine; he would continue to "sport" with his wife like he had always done at home.

"And it came to pass, when he had been there a long time, that Abimelech king of the Philistines looked out at a window, and saw, and, behold, Isaac was **sporting with Rebekah his wife**" (Genesis 26:8). The word "sporting" can be translated as fondling, caressing, romancing, intimacy, hugging and

| Together For Ever

kissing. This is the secret to closeness in a marriage relationship.

Some of the advantages of sexual activities as a sport are that it lowers blood pressure because it is also a stress reducer, reduces risk of heart attack, relieves pain by serving as an enjoyable distraction that helps people focus less on their pain and secondly it helps the body to release endorphins, which are the body's own pain-relieving compounds.

It also **lowers the risk of prostate cancer in men.** The National Cancer Institute researchers tracked 29,342 men and found that the more often the men ejaculated, the lower their risk of prostate cancer. Those who reported 21 or more ejaculations a month during their 20s were 33 percent less likely to develop prostate cancer later in life than those who reported only seven ejaculations per month.

5. Consolation

Sometimes one partner is down and some form of sexual relationship with the other partner is all they need to perk them up. This was evident in the life of Isaac and Rebekah. "Then Isaac brought her into his mother Sarah's tent; and he took Rebekah and she became his wife, and **he loved her**. So Isaac was **comforted after his mother's death**"(Genesis 24:67).

In this we need to be very sensitive to our spouse. The troubled spouse may not say it especially if it is the woman.

Husband, endeavor to use your intuition to know when your wife needs you for this purpose, she may not tell you directly.

HOW TO RE-IGNITE THE PASSION IN YOUR SEX LIFE

Knowing the purpose and advantages of a vibrant sexual relationship with a man and his wife, the question should then be, "What can we do to add that sizzle to, and re-ignite that passion in our relationship?" Well sexual relationship between a man and his wife should not be a quick fix act but an act that starts with intimacy. It starts as soon as you wake up and runs through the day and probably culminates into the act at night.

Here are some pointers that you may need to practice on a daily basis or as often as possible to keep re-igniting the passion in your bedroom.

1. Create a Positive Atmosphere for intimacy

Since in most marriages, the bedroom is usually their play ground, you want to make that bedroom a haven on earth. A place you come in and feel welcome. Arrange your environment in such a romantic way that once you step in you want to cuddle. Change the sheets regularly, have a sweet fragrance plugged in all the time, some erotic candles may not be a bad idea. Cleanness on the part of the couple is also a great turn on. Maintain a clean environment, it's always inviting and adds spice to your sex life.

Ladies it's time to bring out those seductive, sensual and much revealing lingeries to seduce your husband. Make yourself attractive to your husband. A man is attracted by what he sees. After all you are the only one who is permitted to do that. "And they were both naked, the man and his wife, and were not ashamed" (Genesis 2:25). Let him see and feel your body. Give him reason to be intoxicated by your love.

Some other things that set the right atmosphere is writing your spouse a love note, a love poem, sending out flowers, calling on the phone or sending out a text or email just to say "I love you", or telling your spouse how beautiful or handsome he/she is. For ladies, gestures like helping in the kitchen or with the house chores are absolutely quite romantic. Exchanging gifts no matter how small is also a good one.

Let your goal and desire always be to please your spouse. Cast off the idea of selfishness in the room of intimacy and sex because it will only bring disaster. Selfishness will only result in your spouse withdrawing from you. "The marriage bed must be a place of mutuality-the husband seeking to satisfy his wife, the wife seeking to satisfy her husband." (I Corinthians 7:3 The Message).

2. Maintain a regular date night

Date nights do not have to be so expensive as to break the wallet. You can always work within your budget. The idea is not to try to impress but to be all alone with that special someone, your spouse.

It's not about having the fanciest date or the most expensive or elaborate one. They work their magic simply by giving you a chance to catch up with each other and shut out the noise of your busy lives. Here are some ideas that will be wallet friendly:

- Find ideas at your local Chamber of Commerce
- Volunteer as theater ushers and get to enjoy plays, dance performances, and concerts for free.
- Planning romantic lunches out with your spouse at a nice restaurant, always costs less than dinner, or better still a brunch.
- Catch a morning show instead for a more reasonable rate. They are usually less expensive plus the romantic benefit of almost having the entire theater to yourselves.
- If you are unable to afford the theatre, rent a movie, buy popcorn and drink and enjoy the movie at the comfort of your home.
- Take a camera with you on your date. Keep on asking people to take your photo and make it a point to lock lips every time the camera clicks and this can serve as a memory on your next date, after getting the pictures developed.
- Transform your bedroom into a getaway retreat by setting it up as a hotel room (I like this one) complete with number on the door, mints on a freshly made bed (use crisp white cotton sheets), a huge stack of towels in bathroom (for an instant Jacuzzi), nice stationery and

a pen (for writing each other love notes), a bottle of something chilling in an ice bucket, and room service.
- Plan a candlelight dinner at home with your spouse, cook your favorite meal, and let everyone know that this is your time alone.

3. Try something new

Yes you don't have to always fall into the same old regular routine. Explore each other's bodies and try something new. Understand that Sex is an art. Who said that sexual intercourse must take the same shape and position all the time? Try new positions and new styles. The missionary position is not the only one.

Now as it concerns oral sex as many have asked, we need to examine (I Corinthians 7:3-5), " Let the husband render to his wife the affection due her, and likewise also the wife to her husband. The wife does not have authority over her own body, but the husband *does*. And likewise the husband does not have authority over his own body, but the wife *does*. Do not deprive one another except with consent for a time, that you may give yourselves to fasting and prayer; and come together again so that Satan does not tempt you because of your lack of self-control."

From the above scripture, we can say that oral sex (stimulating the partner with the mouth) within marriage would seem okay. However, true love considers the desires of our partner. Therefore, to force our partner to perform an act they are uncomfortable with or consider "dirty" would not be showing true godly love for that person.

Sure a man and woman's body belongs to the other person but this does not mean we abuse the relationship by forcing a desire that the other person is not yet ready to engage in. Clearly for those who are married and may be physically disabled "normal" man on top of woman sex may be impossible. Oral sex and/or stimulation using a finger may provide an avenue for a joyous sexual relationship. If in doubt, pray about it and seek counsel.

Remember the goal is to satisfy your spouse at the end of the day. If married couples will always have a goal and desire to satisfy each other in sexual intimacy, how beautiful that will be. The result is that both will be looking forward to sex and not trying to dodge it or giving up the 'I am tired' excuse.

4. Understand the men and women differences

Someone said that men are like microwaves while women are like crock pots in sexual response. This is for the most part true. A woman lays a heavy emphasis on foreplay because that is how she is wired while the man's emphasis is heavily on intercourse because that is how he is wired. There is no right or wrong in this. The only thing is if you understand that is the makeup of your spouse, then there is need to be sensitive and accommodating of him or her.

Open communication is the key. Ladies let your husband know where your erotic points are and give him chance to explore those. Remember Apostle Paul cautions, "Let the husband render to his wife the affection due her, and likewise also the wife to her husband. The wife does not have authority over her own body, but the husband *does*. And likewise the husband does not have authority over his own body, but the wife *does*." (I Corinthians 7:3-4).

For the sake of the wife, spend time in the foreplay. It's not unusual that a woman will reach orgasm even during the foreplay. If that is the case, the husband has scored a home run and there will still be room for multiple orgasms. So a cue for husbands, try lots of kissing, hugging, and touching in strategic places and you will get the desired response.

Chapter 13

Money and Your Marriage

Many people will tell you that money is the number one reason why divorce happens in a seemingly happy marriage. The point is, couples never got together to learn the principles of money management before they get into marriage. And even after the marriage, not much effort is made in that regard.

The result of this is that each spouse gets into marriage with their preconceived ideas of how to manage or handle money and this ultimately wrecks their family relationship because there is no cohesiveness and no true understanding of money management.

Can money be a uniting factor?

Money can be a uniting factor if couples will handle money as is laid out in the Word of Life. In Genesis, after God made man, He looked at Adam and said, " It is not good (sufficient, satisfactory) that the man should be alone; I will make him a helper meet (suitable, adapted, complementary) for him". (Genesis 2:18 Amplified Bible)

This is where it all began including issues concerning money. So at that point, Eve received an instant job description from God who hired her to do the job. That job is 'helper meet for him, suitable for him, adapted for him and complementary to him.' In verse 24 of the same chapter, God gives them a charge, "Therefore a man shall leave his father and his mother and shall become united and cleave to his wife, and they shall become one flesh". (Genesis 2:24 Amplified Bible)

Therefore this man shall leave all else and be UNITED to this woman as one. From this scripture it is obvious that the intention of their Creator was oneness, including in the area of finance. They are to be UNITED and not divided in ALL areas of their lives without any external interference.

It is very amazing and disappointing these days how married couples have chosen their own areas of oneness. Whereas their Maker made the ONENESS inclusive, they have made it exclusive. And unfortunately what is mostly excluded is sharing their resources together.

I know of many couples who have told each other, we will share everything in this marriage but not money or our resources. Some have even come to a so called compromise whereby, "I don't need to know what you are making just pay so and so bill and that will be fine."

It is not united we stand and divided we bank. Rather its United we stand and Divided in any way we fall. There has to be that unity in all of our finances among married couples both in words and indeed. This is the first step to conquering this number one demon that cause divorce in the home.

Practical steps to achieving unity in finances

Since handling and the use of money is mostly practical and not theory, let us at this time examine some practical steps of using our finances to achieving unity in our marriage.

1. **Talk about your finances.**

Learn to talk freely and regularly about money with your spouse. You talk about everything else why not this one. By discussing the issue of money, you will know and understand each other's view about money especially you will come to understand what money means to your spouse and this will help you both to accommodate each other and to alleviate each other's fears in this area.

2. **Merge your finances.**

There has been so much debate about whether couples should have a joint account or not. Others have concluded that it will be okay to have individual separate accounts and then have one joint account just for paying bills or household expenses. While others have decided that what is mine is mine and what is yours is yours. You keep yours and I keep mine.

Handle your own part of the bills and I'll handle mine and when we have a big project you meet me halfway, 50/50.

We will recommend couples having a joint account because that is the way of oneness and unity as laid out in the word that we read earlier. To this requires that there be a level of trust on each other. You will need to designate one partner who is the more careful one to manage and run the account. Due to the fact that you are both adults and may have personal needs, you may put yourselves on a weekly or monthly allowance and what you do with your allowance is totally up to you.

If at that point you decide to open an account to store your allowance then that will be fine. Have a plan when you get together and review your finances. However, you as a married person will ultimately do what you are comfortable with. Let the goal be oneness and unity in whatever you decide to do.

3. **Be Open with Money.**

The saying that what your spouse doesn't know will not hurt him/her is such a fallacy. Rather, big financial secrets can ruin a marriage. You will be shocked to know that very many couples keep big financial secrets from their spouses to their own detriment.

The belief that he/she will not find out comes bouncing on their faces each time and when this happens, what was ordinarily a good marriage gets ruined because of this. So then what does this tell you? In order to achieve oneness and unity in your marriage, there is great need that both spouses vow to tell each other the truth about money, whether in the area of income or in the area of expenditure.

Remember that your little secret will always find you out and by that time it would have been too late to make amends. There is nothing hidden that will not be revealed. The question is, does your spouse know how much you make and does he/she know what you spend your money on? Be open with money!

4. **Learn to give.**

Part of the reason why couples are not very open with money is insecurity. If you know that you and your spouse have so much money that even in your lifetime you will not be able to scratch one tenth of all the moneys you have, would you be secretive about it? The answer is NO. Therefore one way to ensure enough of money is by giving.

In Proverbs 11:24-26 (Amplified Bible) the bible states, "There are those who [generously] scatter abroad, and yet increase more; there are those who withhold more than is fitting *or* what is justly due, but it results only in want. The liberal person shall be enriched, and he who waters shall himself be watered. The people curse him who holds back grain [when the public needs it], but a blessing [from God and man] is upon the head of him who sells it."

Also in II Corinthians 9:6-7 (Amplified Bible) the bible says, "[Remember] this: he who sows sparingly and grudgingly will also reap sparingly and grudgingly, and he who sows generously [that blessings may come to someone] will also reap generously and with blessings. Let each one [give] as he has made up his own mind and purposed in his heart, not reluctantly or sorrowfully or under compulsion, for God loves (He takes pleasure in, prizes above other things, and is unwilling to abandon or to do without) a cheerful (joyous, "prompt to do it") giver [whose heart is in his giving]."

Having read these scriptures, you see that you cannot afford not to be a giver. You and your spouse will do yourselves a great deal of service to give especially giving your tithes which is one tenth of all your income to where ever God lays in your heart to give it, where you regard as God's storehouse.

Failure to do this has grave consequences as we see in Malachi 3:8-12 (Amplified Bible), "Will a man rob or defraud

God? Yet you rob and defraud Me. But you say, In what way do we rob or defraud You? [You have withheld your] tithes and offerings. You are cursed with the curse, for you are robbing Me, even this whole nation. Bring all the tithes (the whole tenth of your income) into the storehouse, that there may be food in My house, and prove Me now by it says the Lord of hosts, if I will not open the windows of heaven for you and pour you out a blessing, that there shall not be room enough to receive it. And I will rebuke the devourer [insects and plagues] for your sakes and he shall not destroy the fruits of your ground, neither shall your vine drop its fruit before the time in the field, says the Lord of hosts. And all nations shall call you happy and blessed, for you shall be a land of delight, says the Lord of hosts."

5. **Learn to save and invest wisely**.

It is not wise to eat with ten fingers as the elders say. Even if you have a great career, earn a comfortable living and don't have to worry about debt, you could find yourself woefully unprepared for an emergency.

Couples today are under so much stress that anything could tip them. An unexpected pink slip, an accident, illness — anything could throw you off track if you don't have an emergency savings account. All couples should have an emergency stash of three to six months' worth of living expenses held in a safe place, like a money-market fund. Simply knowing it's there can reduce stress, since you know you're not walking a fine line between comfort and catastrophe.

Another thing besides saving that a couple should work on is wise investment. It is advisable that couples sit down and talk about their investment goals and time frames. You could also seek the help of a broker or a financial planner. Whatever your investment choices, review your investments together at least once a year and make sure that, overall, your portfolios balance each other out.

6. **Keep the spending in check.**

Your husband keeps nagging at you that you spend too much — but then comes home one day with a huge smile and — surprise! — A 70-inch flat-screen LED TV. He happily explains how he sealed the "terrific" deal. You're definitely not impressed. Sound familiar?

Spending is the second most common reason why couples fight. What usually happens is that one spouse gets labeled the "spender" and is blamed for skimming all the money out the checkbook. In most cases, however, that's not accurate. It's a known fact that men and women spend the same, they just spend on different things.

Women usually take care of most of the family's daily expenses: the groceries, the bills, clothes for the family —

while men spend on large purchases like LED TVs, cars or computers. The solution here is to identify the real problem, which is that you're both spending money on a tight budget. Then sit down and decide how much money you'll allocate to the daily needs of life, and how much to save for the big purchases. Budget, Budget, Budget.

Spontaneous spending has not helped anyone and it is a threat that you have to get out of. Remember you are accountable for whatever resources God blesses you with. Also remember that the sales are always going to be there. If you don't catch them this time, you can always catch them next time when you are more prepared for it.

Together For Ever

Chapter 14

Maintaining the Family Altar

The altar is where we meet and commune with God. It is that place reserved exclusively for God in our heart and in our house. It represents the presence of God in our house and our reverence for God in our heart. The state of your family altar is indicative of the place of God in your family. The family altar may be a place or a scheduled practice. You may designate a place and a time specific to worship God or several times in different locations in the house.

God is primarily interested in the constancy and continuity of the human race. He made us like him and wants us and our children to remain like him. He wants us to maintain a relationship with him at the altar as the place of keeping the fire in our hearts and our family altar burning. The channel of communication between us and God must be kept open and unclogged at all times.

That is why the first assignment and blessing that God gave to man was for the purpose of ensuring constancy and continuity:

"Be fruitful and multiply" (Genesis 1:28).

The word "fruitful" means to produce life, and to multiply means to increase in number. The Adamic household was therefore the cornerstone of God's plan for pursuing this doctrine of Constancy and Continuity. When Adam was 130 years he became the father of a son in his own likeness and named him Seth (Genesis 5:3).

Again after the pollution of the people in Israel and the restoration of their fellowship with God, Moses restated this doctrine to the Israelites just before they entered the Promised Land, when he said:

"Listen, Israel! The LORD our God is the only true God! So love the LORD your God with all your heart, soul, and strength. Memorize his laws and tell them to your children over and over again. Talk about them all the time, whether you're at home or walking along the road or going to bed at night, or getting up in the morning. Write down copies and tie them to your wrists and foreheads to help you obey them. Write these laws on the door frames of your homes and on your town gates" (Deuteronomy 6:4-9 Contemporary English Version).

The doctrine of **Continuity of worship in the family has three component areas of focus** for those intending to live in accordance with the plan of God.

1. There must be a **Revelation** of God to the children.

2. There must be a wholehearted **Response** to the revelation of God (Acceptance of God).

3. There must be **Responsibilities** toward God (Obedience).

God has designed the family for the execution of His master plan. It is the laboratory where all the theories of the bible are tested and tried. Your household is therefore a mini church with the husband and the wife as the pastor, priest, teacher, prophet, intercessor and congregants. The church at home is unique in that it is a functional 24hrs/7days, year round fellowship.

The curriculum must be focused on knowing who God is, accepting who God is to the family and obeying the principle of life in accordance with God. Parents need to develop strategies for passing on the touch of their knowledge of God to their children in this unique 24hr/7days year round Church. What an opportunity we have to breed the next mighty men of God or the next men of the world. You house is a place for both indoctrination and application of biblical principles.

Studies have shown that children from families where the principles of the scriptures are taught and applied are more likely to maintain their faith than children that were just taken to church on Sundays. This makes the church at home the best place to begin and continue your Christian ministry (I Timothy 3:5**)**.

Maintaining family alter is so central to the plan of God that it has been compared to the relationship between Jesus Christ and the church. As Jesus Christ died to save the church, so should husbands strive to present their families blameless and ready for heaven? Jesus Christ paid the ultimate price for his beloved church and expects husbands to do whatever they can to ensure that the wife and children make heaven. It is both the master-plan and grass-root plan to reconcile every family with God.

Maintaining families alter also gives the members of the family an opportunity to do their ministry. It fosters the right atmosphere for the members of the family to continue in the faith 24hrs/7days and 365 days a year.

In Acts 2:42, the apostles continued in the doctrine of the church, praying, worshiping and practicing their faith under the same roof. Those gifted in vision can minister to the family with it, those who prophesy can prophesy for the family and those gifted in word of worship can lead the family to God.

A strong family alter creates and supports Christian living to the fullest by providing and reinforcing the rules of engagement for every member of the family and guests to follow.

Parents rely on the church to teach their children the way of the Lord but God's plan is for the parents to train their children. While it is good to introduce your children to a vibrant church, parents cannot relinquish their responsibility of raising their own children at home. It amounts to relying on the public television to teach your toddlers.

The local church plays the role of the school in the education of your children. The church is available to your child only when the church is open for church business and is not customized to reach your child alone. Only those that live with their children have the opportunity to observe them and instruct them on the need of the hour.

Together For Ever

Chapter 15

Dealing with Third Parties

"When you invite people into your house they come with their bodies, souls and spirits and they never leave with all their baggage. Before you open your door, consider the doors the stranger might open for your family" – Vic Victor.

God's idea of a family unit is a husband and a wife with their children. Any other person residing or visiting with the family is an extension of the family. It is very important to define your family with such clarity that your interests and boundaries are unmistakable to you, your spouse and all. You can achieve this by articulating your family's rules of engagement to members of the extended family, close friends and everybody else. "He created them from the beginning male and female".

The rule of thumb is to treat your family as an incorporated entity with articles of incorporation or a nation with a constitution. The guiding principle should be; the will of God, self-protection and self- preservation in that order.

This may sound cruel and cumbersome but that is really how our God operates.

The first instruction given to the first husband was leave your father and his mother and cleave to your wife in order for them to become one flesh.

"For this cause a man shall leave his father and his mother and shall cleave to his wife and they shall become one flesh" (Genesis 2:24).

The first point of this statement is that the creator of marriage has laid down the blueprint for marriage –Leave your present baggage behind because you got enough baggage to carry in the new relationship. Take the baggage of your spouse and become one with your spouse. It is always problematic for a man to establish a family without leaving his father and mother.

Two areas of conflict are as follows:

Conflict of Loyalty

When a man is still attached to his father and mother it may present a problem for the new union. The man struggles to balance his loyalty to his father's house and his own house. The situation is further complicated because he wears different hats in both houses. He is a kid in his father's house but a King in his own house. He is conflicted and sometimes forgets which hat he is wearing at different times. When he encounters problems in his house, he calls home for advice and relinquishes his responsibility to the wife.

We also have competing loyalties between parents and spouses. Here we have two personalities that demand the same attention but command different powers. One is losing her grip to power while the other is tightening her grip on power. The tug of war can be excruciating and endless with the parties asserting their claim on every opportunity available. The man is confused while the woman is conflicted. God, the maker of marriage knows it and gave us the solution long before the problem starts. Leave when the motivation is highest, leave before you start a family because you cannot serve two masters at the same time.

Conflicts of Lifestyles:

The man is conflicted between the traditions of his father's house and his house on social matters, spiritual matters and relationship. He experiences stiff resistance from his wife as he tries to introduce some of the old lifestyle to his new house.

For instance I am the 4th child in a family of 6 children and two parents. We had maids and cousins living in our house at all times while growing which made it a bit chaotic at times. Food was not plentiful but always enough for everyone. We hardly had formal dinner since my mother was a business woman and my father was a government worker.

| Together For Ever

When I got married, my wife wanted us to have formal dinners on Sunday afternoons. Good idea but that lifestyle change drove me nuts during the early years of our marriage. I was used to coming home from Church and grabbing whatever was ready. Now I was being required to wait for the table to be set and for everybody to be ready, say the grace and eat with decorum. Good idea to introduce to the family but tough habit to adjust to.

God wants us to establish a new way of life by incorporating some of the things that worked for our fathers and mothers on both sides of the aisle.

The second point to note in the blueprint of marriage is that children and members of the extended family are not mentioned in this manifesto of marriage. Many couples think that their marriage is incomplete without children. But marriage is the relationship of husband and wife while children are the result of that relationship. Your children are in the fulfillment of the command of God for the man to be "fruitful and multiply", and has nothing to make the marriage complete. Your Children were not part of God's solution for your loneliness, but a product of the marriage.

The third point in the blueprint and perhaps more relevant to this discussion is that the road map to successful marriage specifically excludes (at least to some degree) third parties, extended families, friends and foes. The new relationship requires a degree of bonding and exclusivity that cannot be achieved with a divided attention or distracted interest.

It is important for the couple to disengage from all prior associations, affiliations and affinities and thereafter selectively re-engage them in accordance of the new rule of engagement. Do not be shy or equivocate in announcing that there is a new sheriff in town, and he does not accept a plea bargain. The best protection you can give to your family is a sign that says "my spouse and children come first".

Here are just three of the potential problems that the third parties can bring to your marriage:

1. **Criticism:** Some third parties are close enough to evaluate, criticize and question your way of life and your authority. Miriam and Aaron were the closest people to Moses. They were his right 'hand men' and yet his strongest critics. In Numbers 12: 1-16, Aaron and Miriam criticized Moses for marrying a non-believer. They challenged his authority as the prophet of God. The criticism was so strong that God intervened on Moses' behalf and plagued Miriam with leprosy. The prophet Micah says that "...a man's enemies are the men (members) of his own house." (Micah 7:6b Amplified Bible)

2. **Alternative:** Any alternative to the plan of God for your family can become a distraction - **Third parties** can offer you an alternative to the promise of God, especially when things are not working well. Sarai, Abraham's wife offered her maid to Abraham to sleep with him for the purpose of bearing children. This was in spite of the promise of God that Abraham will be the father of many nations. Abraham

accepted the offer and had Ishmael with Hagar (Genesis 16:1-5, Genesis 21:1-2, 9-14).

3. **Terminate your destiny: Third parties** can lead us to abandon our vision and terminate our destiny. If God had not intervened with Ishmael, Abraham's destiny with Isaac would have been affected.

In as much as third parties can cause problems in our marriages, they can also bring a lot of blessings to us. That's why you must leave your family and friends behind when you get married, but you have to visit periodically.

Some blessings that the third parties can bring to your marriage:

1. **Support and Counsel**: Your extended family members and friends can be a great resource for different kinds of support for your family. This support can be emotional, physical and financial for settling down. Although they may not be your mentor, they can provide the same counsel and direction as your mentor. In Exodus 18:19-27 we read about the great counsel that Jethro, the father in-law of Moses gave him about the management of the affairs of the people. Ruth, the daughter in-law of Naomi provided love and affection to Naomi after her husband and her two sons died (Ruth 1:1-17).

2. **Protection and Provision**: Members of your extended family can provide reliable protection for you in time of need. They can also be a source of help when your family needs help. It was Paul's nephew that overhead the plot to kill Paul

and that revelation saved Paul's life and extended his ministry by so many years.

3. Destiny Helpers: Although third parties can and often do distract you from the pursuit of your vision, they can also be used by God as your destiny helpers. Boaz saved David's destiny by agreeing to marry Ruth and also redeeming the debts of Elimelech, Naomi's husband.

For many couples, the process of disengaging from their parents is often difficult and incomprehensible. Some succeed in leaving physically but remain with their parents mentally, spiritually or otherwise. Some have complained that it felt like they were abandoning their father and mother. Others resist the feeling of losing a lifetime of identity. But this is hardly the case.

You are leaving and not abandoning your parents and your true identity is with your new family. That's where your stock is now and should be for the rest of your life. The adage, 'old wine cannot be contained in new wineskin' is well articulated here:

"But no one puts a patch of unshrunk cloth on an old garment; for the   patch pulls away from the garment and a worse tear results.

Nor do men put a new wine into an old new wineskin; otherwise the wineskins burst and the wine pours out and the wineskin is ruined; but they put new wine into a fresh wineskin, and both are preserved"

Together For Ever

(Matthew9:16,17)

This does not mean that couples should exclude other people like parents, siblings, friends and neighbors from their life etc. It means that marriage is a private affair that is celebrated in the public. It also means that the primary focus of the couple must be on how to build an effective team made up of the husband, the wife and their children, and then others.

Bearing this in mind the couple must protect the family first before engaging other people. Your extended family and your friends should not have to guess where you loyalty lies at anything. It should be clear to all that your spouse comes first before everyone else. There is nothing more protective than a sign that says "My spouse and my family come first".

In my house the children know that whatever they share with me or my wife is shared between us at the earliest opportunity. One time my daughter asked me if we "gossip" about them. And I said no because you can only gossip with another person but in our case we are one. Sometimes the children share things they would rather I keep from my wife but I still insist on them sharing with their mom and vice versa.

What do you do before opening your doors for people?

Each couple needs to exercise great caution when deciding to allow other people to visit with the family. Many homes have been ruined by careless open door policy. The peace and tranquility of the family sucked out after a third party's visit or stay. We are unaware that it is both a spiritual matter as well as a physical matter. Ask yourself these three preliminary questions before giving serious thought to inviting people into your home:

1. Will God be pleased with this visitation?

2. Will the visitor add to or remove from the unity and peace of the family; and

3. Will the visitor add to the vision of the family?

Answering these questions objectively and prayerfully will help you eliminate 70% of the potential visitors to your house. If the answer is yes to all three questions then you go to the next phase of the process. **When people come to your house they bring with them their body, their spirit and their soul.** Many of us concentrate on the effect of the presence of the body alone. You should worry about the effect of the spirit, the energy and the aura if you will in your house and over your family.

It may require more intensive prayers before you proceed or seeking counsel from your pastor or minister. The following suggestions are recommended before deciding how to deal with other people especially members of your extended household and strangers.

1. Pray and ask God for wisdom to make the right decision.

2. Detach yourself from sentiments in the decision making process.
3. Focus on pleasing God (as opposed to man) as your main goal in the opening of your doors to anybody.

In Genesis 21 we read about Abraham's anguish in dealing with a third party in his family. The background to the story is that Abraham was married for many years and yet childless and was well advanced in years in spite of God's promise that he will be the father of many nations.

Sarah, Abraham's wife decided to help God out by suggesting that Abraham sleep with her maid, Hagar to see if she could have a child through the maid. This was legal then since maids and slaves were treated as properties. Abraham refused but later gave in and Hagar conceived and had a son Ishmael. A few years later Sarah conceived and had her own son Isaac. Trouble started when Sarah saw Ishmael mocking Isaac and asked Abraham to send Hagar and Ishmael away.

The bible says that "the matter distressed Abraham greatly" (Genesis 21:11). You can say that he was distressed because of the unfairness of Sarah's proposal to send Ishmael and Hagar away. He must have thought that neither he nor Hagar asked for this and Ishmael certainly did not deserve to be abandoned by his own father. This whole thing was Sarah's idea and now she was asking Abraham to clean up her mess.

Although Sarah's proposal seemed unjust in the eyes of man, God approved it because it was in line with his plan and purpose. Abraham obeyed God and complied with the request. Your decision must be one that pleases God.

Secondly, you must detach yourself from sentiments in the decision making process. Abraham sent Ishmael away to the wilderness with only minimal provision.

"So Abraham rose early in the morning and took bread and skin of   water;, and gave them to Hagar, putting them on her shoulder, he it and the boy to Hagar, and sent her away. Then she departed and wondered in the Wilderness of Beersheba" (Genesis 21:14).

How often do we play the role of God in other people's lives? We wonder what will happen to the other person and imagine the worst case scenario if we fail to act. We then act in response to that sentiment. This happened to me in 1995.

That year we invited an old friend and her two children to live with us in our two bedroom and two bath apartment. The apartment was just big enough to accommodate my family of four with the kids sharing the room. Accepting to accommodate the old friend meant going from a family of four to a household of seven. This was definitely going to breach the unity and tranquility of the family.

We had previously introduced her to our friends and Church members when she visited with us a year earlier. Surprisingly when she returned a year later she arranged to stay with one of our friends without informing us. We were deeply hurt but remained calm and cordial. A few months later, her host asked her to leave their house. She was on the verge of becoming homeless when she asked us to accommodate her and her children.

Despite the pastor's advice and against our better judgment we took the woman and her two children into our house, a decision we regret till this day because years of friendship were ruined. Our pastor had advised us to rent an apartment for the friend. Like Abraham, we were deeply distressed by the prospect of this lady and her children going to live at the shelter. We wondered how she will pay her rent and move around since she had no job and no car.

Unlike Abraham, we could not rise up early in the morning to send this woman away with her two children. Trouble started almost immediately she moved in and stopped only after we moved out of the house. The first problem was amongst the children. At that time both our two year old son and our five year old daughter resented the inconvenience of losing their room and hated that the visitors were "always messing" with their stuff.

I was young and lacked the experience to effectively manage the personalities involved. I dismissed my daughter's complaint as childish and reasoned that she needed to learn to share. Years later I realized that whenever my decision affected the whole family, I will at least seek their opinion as part of the decision making process.

Of course there are some potential visitors that do not merit serious consideration and the thought of inviting them to your house should be summarily dismissed. If you are in doubt as to whether your family will be blessed or burdened by your relationship with your extended family, seek counsel from your pastor.

Together For Ever

PART IV

When Marriage Fails.

Together For Ever

Chapter 16

What the Bible Says About Divorce

God's Standard

In Matthew 19:4-6 the bible says, "He answered, "Haven't you read in your Bible that the Creator originally made man and woman for each other, male and female? And because of this, a man leaves father and mother and is firmly bonded to his wife, becoming one flesh—no longer two bodies but one. Because God created this organic union of the two sexes, no one should desecrate his art by cutting them apart" (The Message)

In creation, God made Adam first and then created Eve. He saw that everything He made was good and perfect except that man was alone. So thereafter, seeing the frailty of man, God decided that He would make a woman that is perfectly suited for him and then the completeness and perfection of all creation would come together.

God put this man to sleep and from his rib formed a woman which the man Adam accepted as being part of him. Eve shows up to complete and perfect God's creation. The whole creation was not perfected until Eve was created. It is not necessarily the creation of Eve as a person as opposed to the creation of a help meet for Adam that perfected creation.

God would have had a sigh of relief and greatest achievement when He finally gave Adam a helper suitable for him. So before God, the man and his wife are one flesh and He warns that no one should cut, separate, tear or make imperfect this union, because by doing so, the art or purpose of God is being desecrated. This is God's standard!

What is divorce?

In order to gain a good understanding of this topic, it will be beneficial if we can attempt to delve a little bit into the meaning of the word 'divorce'. Divorce is a word that spells doom when we hear it. It is not a very palatable word. It is what you would not wish even on your worst enemy.

This singular word has wrecked so many lives both young and old. It is a child's worst nightmare. Even the society is adversely affected by this word and the effects of it. So then the question is, "What is divorce?"

Divorce (or the dissolution of marriage) is the final termination of a marital union, cancelling the legal duties and responsibilities of marriage and dissolving the bonds of matrimony between the parties. (Wikipedia)

In so many western countries where monogamy is practiced, it requires a legal/court proceeding to dissolve a marriage. The purpose of divorce then is to *terminate* a couple's marriage.

In order words, it is making imperfect what God has made perfect. No wonder then He says "I hate divorce" (Malachi 2:16). The word hate is a very strong word. God is a God of love but there are few things He actually hates and when He says He hates something then that is exactly what it is. So from off the start we know that God hates divorce no matter the reason for it.

Having acquired an overview of what divorce is, the next question is what *then does the bible say about divorce?* We shall now examine this from the point of view of God, our Lord Jesus Christ and pillars of faith like Moses and Paul.

Moses' take on divorce

One of the earliest discussions of divorce in the bible was made by Moses. "When a man takes a wife and marries her, and it happens that she finds no favor in his eyes because he has found some uncleanness in her, and he writes her a certificate of divorce, puts *it* in her hand, and sends her out of his house, when she has departed from his house, and goes and becomes another man's *wife,* if the latter husband detests her and writes her a certificate of divorce, puts *it* in her hand, and sends her out of his house, or if the latter husband dies who took her as his wife, *then* her former husband who divorced her must not take her back to be his wife after she has been defiled; for that *is* an abomination before the Lord, and you shall not bring sin on the land which the Lord your God is giving you *as* an inheritance. (Deuteronomy 24:1-4)

Together For Ever

In this scripture, a man takes a wife and marries her. This is the normal course of marriage. They are excited and everything is going as planned so far. However, after that marriage that was full of love and oneness, as is the case with most marriages of these days, there comes a twist…what happens?

The husband begins not to like his wife anymore, or in other words she finds no favor before him again, she no longer pleases him – All these emotions are emanating because of one thing. . This reason may have existed before or after the marriage. The fact is that the man did not know it or it did not affect his love for her at the time.

The bottom line is, after the marriage the man begins to resent his wife because according to the various translations of Deuteronomy 24:1, stating the reason for this resentment, it could be that he found something wrong, indecent, disgraceful or something bad with her.

What should a man in this position do? This was the problem that steered Moses in the face. Normally this man, since he no longer likes the woman for one reason or the other would just put her away and send her back to her parents' home. The result is that no one knew when the first marriage ended in case she wants to start a new one.

This became very chaotic in Israel at the time. This was the initial desecration of the institution of marriage. When this issue was brought to Moses to settle, he gave a stipulation, for the very first time since the creation, and his stipulation was that this man should at least give this lady a "Bill of Divorce," and send her away quietly. That was all he had to do.

The woman was required to leave the man's house as soon as the Bill of Divorce touched her hands. No questions, no negotiations, nothing. Remember that Moses took this step, as Jesus will note later in Matthew 19, because of the hardness of their hearts and also under undue pressure from the people.

What then happens after she leaves? Practically, she is now free from that husband and she can get married again to another man. So she comes in contact with a man that loves her and decides to marry her, so far this is good for her. Her sorrows are now replaced with joy and she is happy again.

If after this second marriage the husband starts to dislike or hate her again because of what he discovered she did badly before the marriage, he also has the responsibility of writing her a divorce paper, handing it to her and sending her away from his house.

If this is the plight of this woman, guess what the Bible says about her in verse 4 of Deuteronomy 24? She can never again be remarried to husband number one. There is no make up there. Why? Because it is an abomination before God to do so.

She has already slept with husband number two in the meantime, and for that reason she is now joined together as one with husband number two, and therefore cannot go back to husband number one. As far as husband number one is concerned, she is virtually unclean. According to Moses' law, once a woman is divorced, she can no longer be remarried to her initial spouse, especially if the woman marries another man.

I would infer that she could go back to husband number two if he decides to forgive her and accept her back— nothing wrong with that. The embargo is on husband number one. And it is not necessarily because she got married to husband number two, it is because by inference they have done what husband and wife do naturally— sleep together, therefore they have been joined together.

God's attitude towards divorce

When a man marries a woman and they become husband and wife, God is a witness in that union and it is a covenant/vow that they both get into, such a covenant should not be broken because as they have vowed and as God has witnessed, they are one flesh and no longer two.

And God requires from this union godly offsprings. No wonder why He plainly says "I hate divorce." God also admonishes married people to guard their hearts and not to be unfaithful to their spouse. Don't cheat on your spouse. Don't put away or separate from your spouse.

"God was there as a witness when you spoke your marital vows to your young bride, and now you've broken those vows, broken the faith-bond with your vowed companion, your covenant wife. God, not you, made marriage. His Spirit inhabits even the smallest details of marriage. And what does he want from marriage? Children of God, that's what. So guard the spirit of marriage within you. Don't cheat on your spouse. "I hate divorce," says the God of Israel. God-of-the-Angel-Armies says, "I hate the violent dismembering of the 'one flesh' of marriage." So watch yourselves. Don't let your guard down. Don't cheat" (Malachi 2:14-16 The Message).

In Isaiah 50:1, the Lord Himself was accused of divorcing His own people and selling them. He said, "For your iniquities you have sold yourselves. And for your transgressions your mother has been put away". Again we see another example where divorce happens because someone, in this case a wife, transgresses, sins, does bad things, wrongs her husband, etc, and this gains her a bill or certificate of divorcement.

In Jeremiah 3:1, God takes the position of husband number one. He gets married to his people, Israel, they commit sin, He puts them away in divorce and they go and get married to other men (gods) and now want to return back to husband number one which is God, and He asks, "Why are you trying to come back? Should I take you back? Would that not be pollution in the land?" God divorced Israel because of unfaithfulness, infidelity and adultery (Jeremiah 3:8).

However, the Lord gives the Israelites a chance to come back to Him. He beckons them to come back. He said that "Only know, understand, *and* acknowledge your iniquity *and* guilt--that you have rebelled *and* transgressed against the Lord your God..." (Jeremiah 3:13 Amplified Bible). And God said "I will not cause My countenance to fall *and* look in anger upon you, for I am merciful, says the Lord; I will not keep My anger forever." (Jeremiah 3:12 Amplified). So for God, His demands is, come back to me and admit your guilt and I will forgive you and accept you back. There should be room for forgiveness in marriage. Each spouse should obtain grace from God to forgive each other no matter the wrong.

Jesus discusses on divorce

Matthew 19:3 records, "And some Pharisees came to Him, testing Him and asking, 'Is it lawful for a man to divorce his wife for any reason at all?" The phrase "any reason at all" had its background in the positions taken by two different rabbinical schools of thought headed by two leading Rabbis.

One group, led by Rabbi Shammai, held that you could divorce your wife only where immorality was involved. The other school of thought, led by Rabbi Hillel, said that you could divorce your wife for any reason, and that is the background for this question.

They were asking if He agrees with Rabbi Hillel when he says that any reason is a sufficient reason to divorce your wife. If she burns your dinner, obviously that is a good reason; if she does something you do not like, divorce her! In other words, any reason at all is a sufficient cause for divorce. Just like in the days of Moses.

Together For Ever

When Jesus responds to their question, the Pharisees try to get Him from the other side. So they are really not primarily interested in the truth, but Jesus responds and gives them the truth nonetheless. "And He answered and said, 'Have you not read . . . ?" That question, "Have you not read the Scriptures?" is a blow to these Pharisees who prided themselves in their meticulous study and thorough knowledge of the Old Testament Scriptures.

Jesus understands the motives for their question. "And He answered and said, 'Have you not read, that He who created them from the beginning made them male and female, and said, "For this cause a man shall leave his father and mother, and shall cleave to his wife; and the two shall become one flesh?" ' "(Matt. 19:4). He takes them back to the book of Genesis and says in effect, "Don't you know what it says in Genesis? That is the answer to your question."

On various occasions, Jesus reminded the people that the process of divorce as laid out by Moses: makes it legal to give her a certificate of divorcement and put her away.

This came about because too many people were using this as a cover up for selfishness pretending to be righteous by making the divorce legal. However, Jesus then puts a requirement there… He commands that the ONLY ground to divorce your wife and give her the paper of divorce is if she is found to be guilty of sexual immorality (unfaithful to her own husband).

In this case alone it will be okay for a husband to send his wife away with a paper of divorce. That is the only permissible reason for divorce as far as the Lord Jesus Christ taught.

On the other hand, if there was no sexual sin, promiscuity or infidelity on the part of the woman, Jesus continues to teach, if the husband divorces her "just because", he makes her an adulteress.

This means that you were never married to her in the first place, you were just living in an adulterous relationship with her. Without sexual promiscuity by your wife, you are still husband and wife before God. If she then goes to marry another man, no matter how legal that marriage is, she, being an adulteress, makes the second husband an adulterer.

So a wife can either make herself an adulteress or be made an adulteress by her husband. She makes herself an adulteress if she breaks the sanctity of marriage and now sleeps with other men. In this instance she deserves to be divorced and whoever marries her is marrying an adulteress and commits adultery.

On the other hand, she is made an adulteress by her husband if she is put away for another reason save for sexual infidelity. If she marries any other man in this state, he will still be guilty of adultery because before God, she is still in covenant with husband number one, she has not broken that covenant. But in the earlier case, the covenant of marriage has been broken.

Together For Ever

In Matthew 19:1-12, Jesus succinctly clears any doubts or questions about the stand of heaven as far as divorce is concerned. He responds to the opposition, the Pharisees, who came to trap him with the question, "Is it right for a man to divorce his wife for any reason?"

He reminds them of the very original plan of God, that God made them as one and no one should separate them. Then, the opposition comes with what they think is a more trapping question, 'If that is the case then why did Moses instruct to give a bill of divorce and end the marriage?'

Then Jesus answers them that Moses did that because they were a stubborn people. Jesus pointed out that originally divorce was not part of God's plan for a husband and his wife, Moses stepped it down as a compromise with the people because they did not accept God's teaching or God's original plan. The fact that Moses gave the laws of divorce did not mean that God had that in His original plan.

SO THE ORIGINAL PLAN OF GOD IS ONE HUSBAND, ONE WIFE TOGETHER FOREVER!!!!!

After Jesus' explanation the disciples asked," if those are the terms of marriage, we're stuck. Why get married?" (Matthew 19:10 The Message). To this question of despair, Jesus answers the people—

> 1) Marriage is not for everyone. It is only for those who God has given the ability to accept the principles of marriage and who are willing to

abide by these principles with the help of God, those are the ones qualified to be married.

2) Some people cannot marry because they do not have the ability to become fathers, they are born eunuchs.

3) Some people cannot marry because of what other men put in them.

4) Others have decided not to marry because of the work of the kingdom.

But Jesus said if you are able to accept the teaching /principles on marriage and able to abide by the principle then go ahead and get married. Also Jesus pointed out that if a man divorces his faithful wife and marries another one, that husband commits adultery. (And anyone that marries the one who is divorced also commits adultery). In Mark 10:12 Jesus also adds that if the husband or the wife divorces each other, and marries another they both commit adultery.

Paul's discussion on divorce

In I Corinthians 7:13-15, "And a woman who has a husband who does not believe, if he is willing to live with her, let her not divorce him. For the unbelieving husband is sanctified by the wife, and the unbelieving wife is sanctified by the husband; otherwise your children would be unclean, but now they are holy. But if the unbeliever departs, let him depart; a brother or a sister is not under bondage in such *cases*. But God has called us to peace."

Together For Ever

Here Apostle Paul lays down the biblical principles governing marriages between a believing spouse and an unbelieving spouse who is willing to stay married to the believing spouse.. The believing spouse is not permitted to divorce the unbelieving spouse on account that he/she does not believe.

On the other hand, if the unbelieving spouse decides to divorce the believing spouse, the believing spouse should not stop him/her but should let him/her go. At this point the believing wife/husband is not bound to the unbelieving spouse. The Christian man or woman is free.

In Romans 7:2-3, "For the woman who has a husband is bound by the law to *her* husband as long as he lives. But if the husband dies, she is released from the law of *her* husband. So then if, while *her* husband lives, she marries another man, she will be called an adulteress; but if her husband dies, she is free from that law, so that she is no adulteress, though she has married another man.

So death is another reason permitting a living spouse to marry another person because the living spouse is now under no law not to marry, he/she has been released from the law and can marry whoever God wills for him/her to marry. This is always advisable to do instead of the living spouse to burn with passion and commit sin.

Let us at this time examine some reasons, in this modern times, why married couples divorce and compare these reasons with the discourse above.

Reasons why couple's divorce

About one in every two marriages in the United States will result in divorce or separation. Divorce occurs when, for whatever reason, the married couple makes the determination that they no longer want to be married. But how do things get to this point?

What are the factors that drive people, who were presumably so much in love, to decide to leave each other for good? Well, there could be many reasons for this. Let's examine some of those reasons married couples divorce:

Lack of commitment to the marriage relationship.

Commitment could be lacking in any of the partners because he or she may have married for any reason other than love. The reason could be a feel good one or making a good deal and when it is found that the deal is not what he or she expected, then divorce happens. Besides this, people who are looking for a quick fix solution for marriage are not able to sustain marriage for long.

Lack of open communication between married couples.

Communication is one of the bed rocks of every relationship. For there to be an effective relationship, there must of a necessity be open communication between those involved in that relationship, especially in the case of a marriage relationship. When one partner decides to keep their resentment simmering within, the other partner is usually unaware of what is happening and this usually ends up creating a distance between the couple which ultimately results in divorce.

Abandonment

When one spouse decides to get up and leave their matrimonial home without any notice to the staying spouse and no agreement to this move, it puts a strain on the relationship and causes the spouse that is left behind to opt for a divorce.

Alcohol Addiction and/or substance abuse

Alcohol addiction and/or substance abuse affect marital bliss. This is because there is usually a change in behavioral pattern which makes an adverse impact upon mental peace and physical security and creates resentment for the sober spouse. Ultimately, patience runs out for the sober spouse and he or she asks for a divorce.

Abuse-Physical, sexual, and emotional

Abuse of any kind, whether physical, sexual or emotional is not permitted in any healthy relationship. When those traits are present in a marriage relationship, it is good to get professional help because if not handled properly, the marriage will not only be lost but a life may be lost in the process. So if you are faced with this problem, get help as soon as possible. Some couples have lost their lives to this and some have opted out of the relationship so as to keep their life and sanity.

Inability to manage or resolve conflict

Conflicts will happen in relationships. This is a given fact in every relationship and the marriage relationship is not exempt from this fact. As a matter of fact it is an everyday occurrence in most marriages. It therefore behooves married couples to learn and equip themselves with knowledge on how to resolve conflicts very early in the relationship. The problem is not the conflicts but managing or resolving them. Lack of these skills is the reason many marriages fail.

Differences in personal and career goals

Sometimes couples marry without resolving the issue about their personal goals and career goals. These are very important decisions to make before marriage happens. After the marriage you cannot then wake up and insist on your own goals that never included your spouse in the first place. Some have insisted on their own and have made a shipwreck of their marriage.

Financial problems

Sometimes lack of money or on the other hand, too much of it has weighed down on so many marriages. Financial problems become reasons for divorce, where the couple cannot agree about how finances are to be spent, or where money becomes more important than their relationship.

Mental instability or mental ill health

Challenges of ill health, especially mental health have also posed a reason why some marriages have failed. As much as these challenges can weigh heavily on the healthy spouse, if he/she does not learn how to cope with this challenge, it can get to the point where they opt to leave the marriage.

Unfortunately, the above reasons, though highly convincing in some cases, are not, and cannot qualify as good enough reasons for divorce according to the bible. Is God unreasonable? Not in the least! He is the Master planner for marriage. It was His idea and if you believe that then His idea should supersede our idea. The beautiful thing is that God Himself is able and available to help every marriage succeed.

Conclusion

We must at this point note that God's original plan for marriage is one man one woman living together forever! There was no room for divorce because to do that was to desecrate God's own creation. Moses out of pressure from people of his generation gave in to this pressure but Christ reinstated the original plan.

God Himself makes room for forgiveness if a wife wrongs her husband and vice versa. Jesus adds in His teaching that no divorce should be allowed unless it is only for the reason of adultery. Apostle Paul on the other hand adds more permissible reasons for divorce to include, where the unbelieving spouse decides to leave of their own accord, and where there is the death of one spouse.

Is your marriage at the brink of divorce? Is your spouse threatening to leave you? Knowing what God says about divorce and knowing now that He hates divorce should equip you with the strength and hope to work on your marriage. Your marriage is worth fighting for. There is nothing the devil desires than to have you make the divorce statistics list. It is up to you to withstand his wiles and fight.

This is not time to throw in the towel. It is not over until it is over. This is time for you to pray and intercede for your marriage like you have never done before. "So I say to you, ask, and it will be given to you; seek, and you will find; knock, and it will be opened to you." (Luke 11:9). It is only he who asks that will receive. Solicit the agreement of your pastors and bible believing brethren to agree with you in prayers for the restoration of your marriage. Trust God because He specializes in turning situations around. Your case will not be different!

Secondly, seek counsel from a reputable marriage counselor. Sometimes having someone who is anointed and experienced in what you are going through counsel with you could be the difference between getting a divorce and staying married. Your pastor and ministers in your local church will be good resources for you in this area.

Allow God to work through you and your spouse to bring peace in your marriage. He is the Prince of peace.

Together For Ever

Chapter 17

Picking Up the Pieces

God is the God of restoration. In the book of Joel 2:25 God Himself spoke and said, "The LORD says, "I will give you back what you lost to the swarming locusts, the hopping locusts, the stripping locusts, and the cutting locusts...".". If God Almighty assures you that he will restore all you have lost, it is then your responsibility to have faith in Him as He works you through this phase of your life.

Restoration here means to return you to your original state, as it was in the beginning, as though nothing happened. It is not your business how He does it, yours is to believe in Him to do what He said he will do and it will be so to you according to your faith.

The first thing in the process of restoration is to accept one's responsibilities, actions and reactions to this process of divorce and face the facts. Divorce is a sin before God because it desecrates the marriage relationship from what God intended it to be.

Your first step it to ask God for forgiveness in prayer. The bible says, "If we confess our sins, He is faithful and just to forgive us *our* sins and to cleanse us from all unrighteousness. If we say that we have not sinned, we make Him a liar, and His word is not in us." (I John 1:9,10) When God forgives you, you ought to forgive yourself. Accept His cleansing and be made whole.

The next step is to forgive your spouse. God is able to give you the grace to forgive your spouse for all the hurt and pain that he/she has inflicted on you. Even if he/she has cheated on you, there is also room for forgiveness. However there is much debate on how to forgive, who to forgive and when to forgive. How do you forgive an unrepentant wrongdoer, the man who purposefully harmed you, or the man who disrespected you? What about the repeat offender or the spouse who cheated on you?

The answer to these questions is shrouded in the principles that our Lord laid down. In the parable of the prodigal son, the bible says that "When he [the prodigal son] came to his senses,…", suggesting that the prodigal son was not in his right mind when he asked for his inheritance (Luke 15:17). Again the Lord's prayers for the soldiers that crucified Him was, "Father forgive them for they do not know what they do" (Luke 23:34). If we accept the teaching that "they know not what they do", then the wrongdoing becomes tolerable and the pain is suddenly minimized.

If we understand that every wrongdoing is masterminded by the devil and therefore not intended by the perpetrator, we can then look beyond the offender. This knowledge allows us to make advanced provision of forgiveness for yet to be committed wrongdoings. Until then the prospect of counting 70 x 70 times will continue to be enticing but impossible.

Also make a habit of studying the word of God. Fill your heart with thoughts of the word and of good things and not of bitterness and resentment. "For the rest, brethren, whatever is true, whatever is worthy of reverence and is honorable and seemly, whatever is just, whatever is pure, whatever is lovely and lovable, whatever is kind and winsome and gracious, if there is any virtue and excellence, if there is anything worthy of praise, think on and weigh and take account of these things [fix your minds on them]. Practice what you have learned and received and heard and seen in me, and model your way of living on it, and the God of peace (of untroubled, undisturbed well-being) will be with you." (Philippians 4:8-9 Amplified Bible).

Together For Ever

To order additional copies of

**Together For Ever,
God's Master Plan For Marriage**

Visit the author's website at:
www.twogetherforever.org
Other Books by Authors

The 7 Steps to A Successful Marriage

To contact the authors:
Email: info@twogether4ever.org
Visit the author's website at:
www.twogether4ever.org

Made in the USA
Columbia, SC
14 September 2024